MW01268609

My Journey with God

By Averie Alverson

ISBN -13 978-0-9990297-0-1

"Scripture taken from the NEW AMERICAN STANDARD BIBLE®, Copyright © 1960, 1962,1963, 1968, 1971, 1972, 1973, 1975, 1977, 1977, 1995 by The Lockman Foundation. Used by permission."

Interior Design: Averie Alverson with William G. Alverson
Cover Design: William G. Alverson

Printed in the United States of America

"I will rejoice greatly in the LORD, My soul will exult in my God; For He has clothed me with garments of salvation, He has wrapped me with a robe of righteousness..."

Isaiah 61:10

I dedicate this book to my awesome God, who saved me, cleansed me and then took me on a marvelous journey that has not yet ended. Words cannot describe His infinite unconditional love, His countless blessings, His faithfulness, His patience and the incredible endless surprises He has had for me around every corner. I love You, Jesus, and I pray that this book will enable those who read it to increase their faith and to draw closer to you.

CONTENTS

I.   In the Beginning...   9

II.   God is There...   13

III.   Happy Memories   19

IV.   College Years   23

V.   Army Years   31

VI.   To Dayton   39

    Photo Section   45

VII.   The 1980's   61

VIII.   The 1990's   75

IX.   A New Millennium   89

    Updates   108

Acknowledgements

I would like to express my heartfelt gratitude to my son William G. Alverson, without whom this book would have never been published in this form.

In 2009, I felt directed by the Holy Spirit to write this story about my journey with God for my children. I was to give it to them for Christmas that year. They did not know all the things God had done in my life and in our marriage, because they were not born yet, or were too young to know what was going on. So, I happily sat down at my computer and began typing, with no thought of anyone other than my two children reading it. It was easy. It just flowed from my heart as I recalled all the miracles and blessings, and the direction and provision during hard times that our Mighty God had brought about in our lives!

When the 12" x 12" digital book was completed, I had 3 copies printed – one for Bill and Betsy, and one for me. Immediately, I had requests from friends and strangers to read it, so I began loaning out my copy. After four and a half years of this, and over 50 people having read it, and with a waiting list of people wanting to read it, I heard a prompting from the Holy Spirit to "Print the book in an inexpensive form so more people can have access to it." I had no idea how to do this and knew no publisher would print a book by unknown Averie Alverson. So, I just pondered this for several months wondering how in the world I was supposed to get this done.

Then in January of 2014, I was calling my son about something, and I heard the Holy Spirit say to ask Bill about printing my book while the phone was ringing. I thought, "Why?" When we were done with our conversation, I said to Bill, "I think I am supposed to ask you about printing the book that I wrote for you and Betsy in paperback form." He responded, "Yes Mom, I printed a book for the Flint Public Schools with my professor while attending U of M. I know how to do that and I already have the software on my computer to format it for you." Wow! What an awesome God we serve! I added chapters and story titles, and a few new stories at the end that I thought would be helpful to people facing some of the struggles I had faced and sent the revised text to Bill. After three months and many edits, we finally printed the book.

Thank you, Bill, for the countless hours, and sometimes frustrations while working on this book. The editing could be grueling sometimes, but your patience and desire to help Mom get this done is so appreciated!! I will be forever grateful!

I would also like to thank my wonderful husband Larry, for his never-ending love, support and encouragement from the moment we first met. I cannot imagine my life without you with me all these years!

Chapter 1

In the Beginning...

It all began on May 23, 1949. Mom had to ask Dad to cover her tomato plants the night I was born because it was going to freeze! I had an older brother, Chip, who had been born on January 8, two years earlier. My sister Rudy would follow on May 4, 1953. I was blessed to be born into a nice middle class family with parents who loved each other. We lived the "Leave it to Beaver" life.

Neland Avenue

Our family lived here for the first three years of my life *(photos pg 45)*. I can still remember the large flowers on the wallpaper going up the stairs, the sun room in the back of the house, and the smell of that old garage. Grandma and Grandpa Behler lived across the street from us. Grandma played the piano and the organ at Trinity Methodist Church on Lake Drive. I went to preschool there, and Grandma ended up having a spiritual impact on my life when I was a little older. I was baptized at Grace Episcopal church when 6 months old.

> "But seek first His kingdom and His righteousness, and all these things will be added to you."
> *Matthew 6:33*

Hall Street

We moved to a new house in 1952 *(photo pg 45)*. I grew up here and have many happy memories from those years. We attended Grace Episcopal Church at the corner of Hall and Plymouth. When Mom was a young child, she asked her neighbors who went to church to take her with them. After attending several different churches, she chose the Episcopal church for herself, since her family did not go to church. So now, every Sunday morning, we all drank a glass of juice before leaving for the 9:15 service. Then we came home for a big breakfast - many times it was eggs Benedict which we all loved. Dad even cooked it for us sometimes.

> "This is the day which the LORD has made;
> let us rejoice and be glad in it."
> *Psalm 118:24*

Many days were spent playing with the neighbor kids - outside if the weather permitted. I loved being outside, building forts or snow caves, catching pollywogs and cooking on a coffee can at the pond behind our house, playing games like "kick the can" or "capture the flag", and of course playing with my Revlon doll with the girls. Riding my bike was a favorite too, as well as roller skating. Those were "the good old days."

There is a story that I was not going to include in this book, but I am adding it after Rudy and my friend Vicky said I should. It is about my name - I did not like it while growing up. I dreamed of having the name Wendy. Averie was a very different name and I always had to spell it. When I was sick for two weeks with the mumps, the school sent me a book. When I came to the door, the person looked shocked as they handed me Davy Crockett! They thought Averie was a boy! Then I went downtown to Herpolsheimer's Department Store with my friend Bobbie (Roberta). It was Christmas time and we went to see Rudolph. After talking to me (whoever was behind the scene), they asked if I was there with anyone. I told them I was with my friend. They asked me to wait while they talked to my friend. After she told them her name was Bobbie (Bobby, they thought), they sent 2 boy gifts down the chute to us (guns or something like that). It had happened again! When I became older, I began to like my name because I was the only one!

1952 to 1967

(photos pg 46)

I have believed in God as long as I can remember. I began saying my prayers at a young age every night after I got into bed. I started by praying the Lord's prayer and then would add what was on my mind at the end. I tried not to ask for anything personal, though. I thought that it was selfish to do that, and God might not like it. I don't think I ever forgot to pray - it was such a part of my life. No one really talked about God to me in everyday life, but I was aware of Him much of the time, especially when I was outside in nature. I enjoyed talking to God while in the woods or sitting by a lake. He was my best friend. For some reason, though, I never talked to any person about Him. Maybe that was because people almost never talked about God to me. The only place He was mentioned was usually in church.

> "For the eyes of the LORD move to and fro throughout the earth that He may strongly support those whose heart is completely His..."
> *2 Chronicles 16:9*

Unfortunately, I was a very sensitive soul, and when I got older, I felt rejected by Rudy and Chip, who were close. I figured out in my 30's why they "didn't like me." You see, when I was growing up, I was a "rule obeyer." I was always trying to be good and do the right thing. I respected authority (teachers, parents, police etc.) and felt everyone should obey the rules. I got decent grades in school, and kept my room neat and tried to please my parents. I thought I was normal, but as my husband told me much later, I was definitely NOT the norm. Rudy and Chip were normal - their rooms were messy, they struggled with grades, and usually got into more trouble than I did. No wonder they didn't cozy up to their "goody two shoes" sister! So, let's just say they did not make life easy for me.

There are two people that made a difference in my spiritual life *(photos pg 47)*. The first one was Mrs. DePew. She was my second-grade teacher and she gave us all a prayer reminder. It was like a large sturdy bookmark that had a picture of Jesus on the top, and a white cross underneath His picture. When you turned the lights off at night, the cross would glow a pretty purple, and it would remind you to say your prayers. I loved it and hung it right by my bed.

The next person was my Grandma Behler. Grandma is one of two people in my life who talked about Jesus as a real person, who could be your friend with you every day of your life. She always had the Christian radio station on and her "Daily Word" on the kitchen table. The moment I was born again, I remembered her and knew that she was born again too! Unfortunately, she died one month before I made that decision, so I was not able to tell her. One of my vivid memories is of me sitting on the piano bench next to her, while she looked down at me and sang and played, "There's not a friend like the lowly Jesus, no not one, no not one..."

Just a word about my Grandpa Behler...I loved being in my Grandpa's presence - I felt so safe and loved whenever I was with him. Sadly, he died when I was just seven.

"Permit the children to come to Me... for the kingdom of God belongs to such as these."
Mark 10:14b

Chapter II

God Is There Even When We Don't Know Him Yet!

Even though I believed in God, I didn't really know God. When I tried to read the Bible on my parent's bookshelf, I just couldn't understand it. I believed He existed, I prayed to Him, and I knew He loved me, but I was still dead spiritually. I couldn't truly hear Him speak to me, and I did not have a close friendship with Him. However, I now know He was very involved with my life, even then. I will be sharing many stories of how He has been there for me before and after I gave my life to Him.

When I was young, I had a Revlon doll that had lots of clothes and furniture. One of my pieces of furniture was a rocking chair *(photo pg. 46)*. Others had beds and tables and wardrobes, but no one had a rocking chair like mine. I treasured it. One day, when I got home from Jan Schaubel's house after playing dolls with her, I could not find my rocking chair anywhere. I searched the house high and low, called Jan to see if I left it there, or if it had fallen out of my bag on the way to the car, and asked my family if they had seen it. They helped me look, but no one found it. In the early evening, I walked upstairs to my room, and there it was - just sitting in the middle of my bed! How did it get there? No one in our house had put it there! Chip told me God must have put it there. I immediately agreed with him, and it made my faith in God grow even more. To some it may seem silly to think that God cares about a doll's rocking chair. Well, He probably doesn't care about the chair, but He does care about little girls who want to know Him and are seeking Him the best way they know how. That incident is still very clearly etched on my mind......

> "Where can I go from Your Spirit?
> Or where can I flee from Your presence?
> If I ascend to heaven, You are there;
> If I make my bed in Sheol, behold, You are there."
>
> *Psalm 139:7-8*

The Search Continues...

As I mentioned earlier, being sensitive did not serve me well. If I could have laughed things off and not taken everything so seriously, then maybe I wouldn't have developed such low self-esteem over the years. Many things happened to me that added to my feelings of inferiority, but I will just mention a couple here. When I was about nine years old, one of the "cool" girls invited me over to play after school. I was looking forward to it, but we never made it to her house. To get there, you had to cross a swampy area on a sewer pipe that rose above the water. It was winter and the water was partially frozen. When in the middle of the swamp, she began to push me onto the ice which began cracking. I was terrified, but eventually got away from her by slipping out of my coat that she was hanging on to while pushing me. Then when I was eleven, my best friend of several years, Bobbie, (we did everything together and had such fun) told me on the way to school one day that she was not going to be my friend anymore because she wanted to be with the "cool" girls. Of course, this was another blow to my fragile self-image. We never were friends again, and she was never a "cool girl."

One place that has many great memories is Camp Newaygo on Pickerel Lake. I went there from 5th grade through 9th grade during the summer. We were outdoors a lot, camping, swimming, canoeing, etc., which I loved. During my last year there, our tent was in charge of the worship service one Sunday. The group decided to use a poem I had read and added my own thoughts to as the theme for the service. I felt so honored during the service held at the beautiful outdoor chapel on Pickerel Lake.

Camp Worship Service

World, I am youth.

I am young, strong, and beautiful.

I am perfectly made to do the tasks of mankind.

I am always striving for perfection.

I am faced with the problems of preparing myself to be the leaders of my generation.

My mind is constantly expanding in spirit, moral values, faith, maturity, intelligence, hope, and love.

Life itself means more to me with the dawn of each new day.

The world is a mess with its wars, its poverty, and its wastefulness, but I am told to follow the footsteps of my ancestors.

All my life I have believed that the world was created by God, but now I am being taught that it was not.

I am told that emotions and confusion are a part

*of growing up, but when I become emotional
or confused, they tell me not to act like a child.*

*I am told that youth is wonderful, but I am frowned upon
because I am a teenager.*

*I feel the need to help others who are not as fortunate as I am,
but they tell me to do nothing for anyone unless I am paid.*

*I am told when I am troubled to talk to someone,
but when troubles come, no one is there.*

*I am told the warmth of a friend is necessary for happiness,
but they tell me not to trust anyone.*

*I am expected to be the greatest of tomorrow,
but I am told I am the worst of today.*

The world overwhelms me, I'm confused.

My mind does not have the answers, I'm afraid.

There's no one to help me, I'm lonely.

I'm thinking of me alone. I'm selfish.

But amid my searching, one fact shines bright.

*If I believe in myself and my ideals, and I strive for what I want in life
-- the confusion will no longer seem so real,
and I will succeed!*

"The LORD gives wisdom;
From His mouth come knowledge and understanding.
He stores up sound wisdom for the upright..."
Proverbs 2:6-7

As you can see from this poem, I was a typical teenager of the 1960's. There were a lot of new ideas out there, many values were being challenged, and many adults were frustrated with the younger generation. I have wondered what it was like for those who knew God and were in Bible teaching churches - was it the same for them?

I remember sitting in my church, and looking at the huge mural on the wall behind the altar. Jesus was the largest and central figure, but there was also a stream, animals and other people. *(photo pg 48)*. During some of the services, I would just sit there and look at Jesus and ask Him, "Who are you? I just don't understand this dying on the cross for my sins. Please show me who you are." I guess you could sum up my spiritual mindset at that time by saying I was confused and bored with church.

> "Jesus said to him, 'I am the Way, and the Truth, and the Life;'"
>
> *John 14:6a*

Chapter III

Happy Memories

My happiest memories of growing up were during the elementary school years. Most years our family took a vacation together, usually to some place that was new to us. I absolutely loved seeing new places. These trips were usually during spring break *(photo pg 46)*. I have memories of traveling to New York, Boston, Florida, Biloxi, Mississippi, Williamsburg, and Washington DC. Of course, my favorite trip was a six-week trip we took out west after stopping in Cleveland for my Aunt Donna's wedding. We went west on the southern route through Denver, Colorado Springs, Mesa Verde, Hoover Dam, Las Vegas and Disneyland. We then traveled north through Sequoia National Park and Yosemite Park to San Francisco. We returned home through Reno, Lake Tahoe, Salt Lake City, Yellowstone, and Mt. Rushmore. What an incredible trip! This love of travelling would soon take me on many mission trips around the world.

I also have great memories of our cottage in Newaygo in the summertime. My favorite pastime there was catching turtles - usually painted turtles, but some were snapping turtles - yuk! I was also an avid water skier - so fun! Especially in the evenings when the lake was as smooth as glass!

Jr. High Years

Junior High was a very difficult time for me, as I suspect it has been for many kids throughout the ages. I was the girl in our class to develop physically long after everyone else. This had its disadvantages! The worst thing was that many of the boys in my class picked out the nick name, "Board", for me because I was so flat-chested. I felt so humiliated whenever they would laugh and call me that in the halls. I tried out for cheerleading in 7th and 8th grade, but it was pretty much a popularity contest, and I really didn't have a chance.

During my Jr. High years, I continued to pray and talk to God a lot. By now Chip and Rudy were beginning to "gang up" on me a little. I felt like such an outcast everywhere. I remember hearing Mom and Dad arguing one night after I was in bed - they never argued. This scared me, and I decided that if they got a divorce, Chip would go with one, Rudy would go with the other one, and I would go to an orphanage. What a silly thing to think, but it is amazing where our imaginations can take us.

There is one experience where I truly believe God was very present at the end of 8th grade. The try-outs for the freshman cheerleading squad were held after school one afternoon at the high school. The Varsity Cheerleaders came to the Jr. High for several weeks to teach us the cheers and prepare us for the try-outs. Everyone would try out with a partner, and perform 3 cheers, 2 chants and then do the splits. During my last class that day, I was called out of class and told that I would have to try out alone because my partner, Jan, did not meet the grade requirements for being a cheerleader. This was a good thing for me, since Jan was not very good, and we would not have been in sync. That would make me look bad too. I had spent quite a bit of time praying the night before. I wanted so badly to make it but knew I wouldn't and asked God to help me be a good loser. As a matter of fact, I had told Bonnie, the varsity cheerleader helping me, that I was not going to try out, but she insisted that I do so because she said I was very good. The others in our group agreed with her, so with their encouragement, I tried out.

Well, after school, we all headed over to the high school auditorium, and the try-outs began. Everything happened just as we were told, but when I did the splits, my shorts ripped right up the seam from front to back! I'll never know if anyone heard the rip like I did. I was concerned about going back on stage if I were "called back" which is what always happened next, after the judges left for their first consultation. However, when the judges returned, to everyone's surprise, there were no call-backs, and they announced the new squad in alphabetical order: Marcia Basinger (after which everyone screamed), Averie Behler (which I did not hear because of the screams for Marcia), and Julie Bennett. I began looking for Julie and Marcia to congratulate them when Jan came and congratulated me! That's how I found out that I was a Freshman Cheerleader!

High School Years

My high school years were no better than my junior high years when it came to my self-esteem. The guys came up with a new nickname for me: "Ovary". I felt humiliated every time I would hear them laughing while they said, "Hey Ovary!" in the halls. I never dated anyone in my high school. Being a cheerleader was huge in my life, because it was the one thing that gave me any sense of value as a person. I truly believe that God gave cheerleading to me *(photos pg 47)*. I made the squad all 4 years, which was very unusual at our school and I loved every minute of it! During these years, I continued my prayers every night. I collected poems that were meaningful to me in a binder (and even some that I wrote myself). I continued to enjoy my conversations with God even though I saw Him as this God that was way up there somewhere. Many years later, while meeting with a friend from high school, she asked me if it bothered me when the boys called me "Ovary" from the stands while I was cheering in high school. I had never heard them! God had protected me! I never ceased to be amazed at His love and care for His children!

"...You are a God who sees..."

Genesis 16:13

Turns in the Road

The first turn came when I went on a few dates with Dave Roberts. He was a great guy and we ended up being good friends. However, it was his mother that had more influence on me. She was a Baptist, and was the only person other than Grandma Behler that talked about Jesus as a personal friend in her life. She shared many biblical truths with me. I wasn't ready to grasp it all yet, but she was planting more seeds in my spiritual life.

Then, at the end of my senior year, I was registered at University of Michigan for college in the fall. However, the place to go for spring break that year was Nassau (not the traditional Ft. Lauderdale). Mom and Dad agreed to chaperone me, Marcia Basinger and Julie Bennett on a trip there. I had no idea how this trip would change the course of my life. With three days left on our trip, I met Bob Hall. We were together every minute of the next few days until we left. A couple of weeks after we got home, he surprised me by driving 12 hours from Kansas University to visit me for the weekend. I then flew to KU for a weekend as a birthday gift in May. I stayed in one of the freshman dorms and fell in love with the beautiful campus. I applied to KU when I returned home and received my acceptance in June. Mom and Dad were disappointed because they and my grandfather and other relatives graduated from Michigan. In the end, however, they ended up liking the campus and the feel of the school - much like Michigan when they were there. I never dated Bob when I got to KU, but I would meet my wonderful husband there a few years later. I believe it was God who arranged this turn in my life.

Chapter IV

College Years

Mom and Dad drove me to KU in the fall. When they left, I felt a freedom I had never felt before - a new place where I had no reputation and no one knew me. It was like I was starting out fresh. I really enjoyed my first year while a lot of traditions were still in place at KU. My sophomore and junior years (1968-1969) saw many changes on the campus: protests, drugs, the Student Union was set on fire and the end of many traditions that I thought were fun. There was a lot of pressure to have sex on dates, and even though I thought I should wait until I got married, no one had ever told me why. I ended up pregnant my junior year. This was a huge event that totally changed my life, so I am going to share at length about it here. This is my story…

I felt like I was in a dream. This couldn't really be happening to me, could it? It was 1969, and I was home to celebrate the Christmas holidays with my family in Michigan. But something was wrong - very wrong. My period was two weeks late, and now even the thought of food, let alone the smell or the taste of it, made me extremely nauseated. "I just can't be pregnant!" I kept thinking. "Not now, with only a year and a half left before I earn my business degree. After all, Jim and I had sex only a couple of times," I rationalized, "and he used a condom!" When I returned to school, the test at the university clinic only proved what I already knew in my heart was true. I was twenty years old, a college student, unmarried, and pregnant. After spending almost an

23

entire day sobbing continuously, I pulled myself together so I could think the situation through. Since Jim and I were only friends, marriage was out of the question. Abortion was generally illegal in the United States at that time, so I decided to have my baby and put it up for adoption. I would only miss one semester of school, if any, and could start up again in the fall, after the baby was born. I felt good about this plan and was hoping my brother in Colorado would help by providing a place to stay for the summer months before the baby was born. It wasn't long, however, before I discovered that others eager to help, had a "better" plan. The first suggestion came from the minister at my church in Michigan. He gave my family the details for obtaining a legal abortion in England. Then my roommate told me how I could obtain a legal abortion right there in Kansas. Her father, a physician, would help me get the necessary papers. So, it was decided. I would have an abortion at the University Medical Center. "This must be the best decision," I thought as I went over it in my mind. "My parents, my brother, my roommate, a physician, Jim, and even the church, all think this will be an easy, quick solution to a difficult problem," I reasoned. "As soon as it's over, I can forget about it and get on with my life, never having to think about it again." Soon, however, I would discover how wrong I was.

"...where sin increased,
grace abounded all the more."
Romans 5:20b

I returned home to my apartment eager to start the new semester. Jim and I were still friendly, but we never went out again. Neither did we mention the abortion, now that it was over. Something very strange was happening to me, though. I kept feeling this intense desire to be a mother! "What in the world is wrong with me?" I kept asking myself. "I don't want to be pregnant! I don't want to have a baby out of wedlock!" As I tried to decipher these strange thoughts, I began to feel something like a physical pain deep within me whenever I felt this yearning. Then I began to have real physical pain. It became so severe that I wasn't sure if I could drive myself to the clinic. After arriving at the clinic, I was diagnosed with a spastic colon, most likely caused by the stress of the abortion and the resulting mourning for the aborted baby. I remained in the hospital two weeks before I was released. Since I had missed two of the first three weeks of the semester, and since I was in a weakened condition, I decided to go home. I was so relieved to get away from that place, and I immediately felt better once I left. It was easier to put everything behind me without all the familiar reminders!

Dream Come True

In the summer, I returned to school to resume my education. The spastic colon surfaced again as all the memories returned, but I got into the swing of things and began doing just fine, although the abortion was never far from my thoughts. I met Larry Alverson in one of my business classes, and after our first date on November 3, 1970, we were inseparable. I went home for Christmas vacation once again, but this time I was exuberant with news of my engagement. What a difference from the previous year! Larry and I were married August 14, 1971 at Grace Episcopal Church *(photos pg 48)*.

"...every perfect gift is from above..."
James 1:17

Bringing Larry into my life is probably the second greatest gift that God ever gave to me (the first being born again)! Although I had made some strides in my self-esteem during my college years, it was still quite fragile and I was still very withdrawn and quiet. Larry loved me so completely and unconditionally, that he was the best thing that could have ever happened to me. He certainly isn't perfect, as none of us are, but he was never threatened by my developing strong personality, and encouraged me to pursue whatever I enjoyed. I have often noticed other husbands - wonderful Christian men that I appreciated - but men who were less secure than Larry, or men that were perfectionists or could be more demanding than Larry ever was of me. I think I could have easily been crushed by someone other than Larry - he was just what I needed, and God knew it. I didn't even feel the romantic love that people usually feel when dating seriously. I just had a very real peace and knew that this was the person I was supposed to marry. I remember thinking the week of our wedding how strange it was that I was so peaceful without the romantic "butterflies." I believe it was God leading me. I still did not know Him, but He knew I was searching and my heart was toward Him.

Born Again

After the wedding in Grand Rapids, we returned to KU where I had one semester left and Larry had three. We rented a little two-bedroom apartment in a four-plex near campus. After graduating in December, I took a job at the Student Union Bookstore on campus and we decided to try to have a baby. I would finally be able to satisfy the inexplicable yearning I had experienced ever since the abortion. After two weeks of rush with students buying their books, the manager of the bookstore told me that he wouldn't be needing me because attendance was down the 2nd semester. Tomorrow would be my last day. He had told me this might happen when he hired me, but God had other ideas!

When I arrived at work the next morning, the manager (a cocky young guy), stood next to me looking at the floor and shuffling his foot as he said, "I don't know why, but I am going to keep you on." He may not have known, but God knew why. You see, Jeannie, the cashier who sat next to me, was a beautiful gal about my age who looked like the typical hippie of that era. She was angry and disappointed with her life. She had wanted to go to college, but became pregnant when she was 17 and was now separated from her husband, and the single mom of two boys. She was jealous of the students she was waiting on. One month after I started working there, her life was totally transformed! She became happy, she was nice to everyone, her husband came to take her to lunch and they looked at each other with love in their eyes. Her whole countenance changed! She was glowing! I asked what had happened to her and she told me she had become a Christian. I thought to myself, "Became a Christian? Well, I am a Christian and it doesn't make that kind of difference in my life."

As the next few months went by, her new attitude and glow did not diminish. She began using the term "born again," which I had never heard before.

> "Jesus answered...Unless one is born again he cannot see the kingdom of God."
> *John 3:3*

In the meantime, since the first of the year I had an intense desire to finally know who Jesus was. Larry took me to a movie called "Prince of Peace," but it was dubbed and in black and white and kind of boring. Then we watched King of Kings on TV at Easter time. That was a bit better, but I still didn't understand.

Then in June, Larry left for ROTC summer camp for six weeks. The day he left, I found out from my doctor that I had a tumor the size of a grapefruit in my abdomen. Four days later, June 21, 1972, I met with the cashiers after work for some fellowship at Eleanor Gilchrist's house. Near the end of the evening, I asked Jeannie what she meant when she said, "born again." She explained how we have all messed up and come short of God's holiness. No man had been able to live a perfect life and pay the price for our sin, so Jesus did! When He died on the cross, He was taking the punishment that we were supposed to receive. When we are born the first time, we are born physically. When we are born again, we are born spiritually.

She then said that God loved me just the way I was! She told me that I didn't have to become "good enough" or perfect to come to Him! Wow! I had spent my whole life trying to be good enough for everyone and it never worked. Here was someone who loved me just the way I was. This was music to my ears!

The final thing she told me was that Jesus was sitting on the edge of His seat just waiting for me to ask Him to come into my life! I could hardly wait to leave so I could go home and pray. When I finally got to my car, my hand was shaking as I put the key into the ignition to start the car. As soon as I got into bed, I prayed as always, but this time it was a different prayer. I asked God to forgive me for all my sin and I listed everything that I could think of, including the abortion. I then asked Him to come into my life and take control. I fell asleep without being afraid for the first time since Larry had left (you know, all those noises you hear when you are alone.)

When I got out of bed in the morning, I felt very light, like a heavy load was taken off my shoulders that I didn't even know had been there! The next weekend, I went to visit Larry at summer camp and told him what I had done. He was furious! He did not want me loving God more than Him! He did not want a religious fanatic for a wife! Well, the hater of debate that I am, I did not argue with him. My new friends showed me 1 Peter 3 and told me that I didn't have to "convert" him. All God expected me to do was to be a good wife, show him God's love and pray for him, which I did. God took care of the rest! Larry wanted to be #1 at summer camp. He was #2 and the # 1 guy was a Christian and gave all the glory to Jesus. Then a major general came to speak at his graduation and he too was a Christian. This was challenging Larry's perception of who Christians were. He thought they were old ladies and alcoholics - you know, people who needed a crutch. They certainly were not strong men who had it all together like he did. He went back to work at Goodyear Tire when camp was over, and the guys he'd known there for 4 years began talking to him about God and giving him books and tracts. They had never done this before!

Finally, after reading "The Late Great Planet Earth" by Hal Lindsey, Larry was riding back to campus to go to his weightlifting class when God "showed up in his car." He began crying and had to pull over to the side of the road and give his life to God, too. It was only two months since my own experience. What a blessing! I could see it on his face when he walked in the door of our apartment. Our lives were miraculously changed forever!

Remember when I said that I never felt that romantic love for Larry. Well, the minute he walked in the door, he told me what had happened. Then we hugged, and while we stood there in the doorway hugging, I felt buckets of love being poured over me for him! It was incredible! I believe, in that moment that we were intimately connected, spiritually. Then I knew what Genesis 2:24 meant. "For this reason a man shall leave his father and his mother, and be joined to his wife; and they shall become one flesh."

Remember the tumor that the doctor had found? Well, my new Christian friends prayed for me before my next doctor's appointment at the KU Med Center. When the KU medical student examined me, he looked confused, left the room, came back and examined me again. Then the doctor examined me - They could find no trace of the tumor!

Baptized

It was a group of hippies that had led Jeannie and her husband Terry to the Lord. They had rented a house one block off campus, called it "The Mustard Seed" and held a Bible study there every Tuesday night. Since I went to church growing up and never heard of being born again, I thought maybe churches didn't know about this yet, so we just went to the Bible study. There were only about 6 of us when we started going to the Bible Study that summer. We were baptized in Potter's Pond on campus (photo pg 48). Larry and I were holding hands while one of them stood on each side of us and we were baptized together. It was great! I am sure God was smiling!

> "...Repent, and each of you
> be baptized in the name of Jesus Christ..."
> *Acts 2:38*

By the time we left KU in December, the Tuesday night study was running between 60 and 80 students. Our teacher, Bob Mendelsohn, was a born again Jew who had rabbinical training and knew Hebrew. He was a great teacher. Other ministries like Campus Crusade that did not believe in the Baptism in the Holy Spirit were also on campus. Bob always told us not to argue, but to love one another. We were all a part of the body of Christ. It was a great foundation for our new faith that has served us well over the years. There was an article in the Lawrence paper in the early 1990s about a church called "The Mustard Seed." Our Bible study had merged with a group of professors having Bible study after we left, and then formed a church. The article mentions the church's small beginning in the summer of 1972 with six people - that was US!

Chapter V

Army Years

We left KU and went to Ft. Benning, GA where Larry attended Airborne, Jumpmaster, and Ranger Schools. Larry kept his Bible wrapped in a "fold-over" baggie during Ranger School while he was in the swamps. Somehow God kept that Bible dry even when everything else he owned was soaked. We then went to Ft. Sill, Oklahoma where he attended Artillery Officer Basic Training. We met some Christians there who told us that some churches did know about being born again. We went with them and loved their little church. There is another very important biblical principle that we learned at Ft. Sill. I was in the car with my friend Leah one day when I mentioned we couldn't seem to make ends meet financially. She asked me if we were tithing and I said, "What's that?" She explained that God owns it all, but only asks us to give Him back 10%. If we are faithful to Him, He will meet all of our needs. I went home and told Larry about it and we began tithing that Sunday and have never stopped since. We started tithing on our net income, and then decided it should be on our gross income, before taxes. Leah was right! God has certainly met all our needs, even when we could not see how He possibly could. Many stories of His provision are included in this book!

> "Will a man rob God? Yet you are robbing Me!
> But you say, 'How have we robbed You?'
> In tithes and offerings."
> "Bring the whole tithe into the storehouse..."
> *Malachi 3:8, 10*

Ft. Bragg, NC

After three months at Ft. Sill, we drove to Ft. Bragg, North Carolina for Larry's first permanent assignment in the 82nd Airborne Division. My relationship with God was growing and I prayed about everything, including the army quarters that would be assigned to us. They were 900 square feet, 2 bedroom houses with a car port *(photo pg 49)*. I was so excited to have my first real house instead of an apartment. They came with either a picture window in the living room, or 2 smaller windows. I asked God for a house with the 2 windows like the house I grew up in, and not one next to the Nills. They had big orange letters spelling their name over their door and plastic flowers in their yard. But, I also asked God to pick out the best house for us because He always knows what's best. After three long months, we were finally assigned a house and we drove over to see it immediately. It was kitty corner to the Nills and it had a picture window. God knew that I would love the picture window, and that I would especially enjoy the only private back yard in the housing area because there were several trees surrounding it. All the other yards had no trees and were open to each other.

I was learning how our Heavenly Father really does know best! I met my first close Christian friend, Georgianna, at Ft. Bragg *(photo pg 49)*. We became Tupperware dealers together. As you already know, I was very shy and had a hard time talking to people (I was so afraid I would be laughed at), so God used Tupperware to help me gain confidence in this area. I absolutely loved Tupperware and not having stale food anymore, so I had no problem telling people about it and I did very well selling it. It is amazing how God knows how to pull our gifts and talents out of us. I hated speech in both high school and college, but I had a gift for speaking in me that I didn't even know about. This helped me tremendously as I began to share Jesus with others.

> "Go therefore and make disciples..."
> *Matthew 28:19*

When I first met Georgianna, I didn't think we would become close friends. However, when the four of us (including our husbands) discovered that we were all Christians that had experienced salvation and the baptism in the Holy Spirit about the same time, we became very close friends! It is amazing how a spiritual connection deepens a friendship beyond the ordinary. Georgie and I talked on the phone for an hour or two every day, mostly about the Lord and the army. You see, she and Tim lived off-post and we lived on Ft. Bragg, and our husbands took the only car to work every day about 5 am. Occasionally, one of us would take him to work to have the car for the day. We are still very close today even though we have never lived near each other since Ft. Bragg.

About a year before we left Ft. Bragg, Tim was transferred to Ft. Stewart, Georgia. I cannot tell you how much I missed Georgianna and all our talks. One afternoon, I was sitting on my bed and talking to the Lord. Larry was in the field for a week or two and I was very lonely. I told the Lord how much I missed my friend. I heard Him say to me in my spirit that He wanted to be my best friend, but I didn't have enough time for Him because I spent it all with Georgianna. That really touched my heart. I try not to let any person or thing in my life take His place - it is such an easy thing to do without even realizing it.

> "Trust in the LORD with all your heart
> and do not lean on your own understanding.
> In all your ways acknowledge Him,
> and He will make your paths straight."
> *Proverbs 3:5-6*

Shortly after moving into our quarters, I met Lou Anderson, an Assemblies of God Chaplain's wife. She was teaching a Bible study in her home and I was thrilled to be able to attend it. We were studying prophecy which was very helpful to me. It began in Genesis 3 and went through the entire Bible. I was praying a lot at this time for Larry, "Lord, make Larry pray with me, make him go to Sunday night church, etc."

One morning when I was praying this way again, the Lord spoke to me, "Averie, why are you so worried about what Larry is doing when you are not doing what you are supposed to be doing?" This was a shock to me, but when I thought about it, I had no clue what a Christian wife was supposed to do. I had a great example of a domestic mom (no one's mom did more than my mom), but what does a born again wife act like and do? I told the Lord that morning that I would not tell Larry what to do anymore (God said the Holy Spirit could not get a word in edgewise to Larry because I was saying too much). I asked Him to please show me what I was supposed to be doing. Amazingly, when I went to Bible study a few days later, Lou said, "We are going to set aside this study for a while and we are going to study the Philosophy of Christian Womanhood." Wow! God is so faithful.

That Bible study totally changed my life and my marriage. God showed us the plan He had for husbands and wives in marriage (the man's role and the woman's role.) I learned so much about being a godly wife that I could apply to our marriage. I read other books on the subject as well, and completely stopped nagging Larry. About 6 months later, Larry began on his own to do many of the things I had wanted him to do. It was now his idea and not mine. Then, the following spring, while we were walking Brandy, our golden retriever, in the park, Larry turned to me and said, "I am so happy for you. You seem so much happier than you used to be!" He didn't say he was glad I wasn't nagging him anymore, but that he was glad I was happy! That was a great blessing! I was just beginning to learn how faithful God is to us when we obey Him.

"...We must obey God rather than men."

Acts 5:29b

Sometimes He asks us to do things that seem too hard, or we just don't want to do. But if you do obey, the blessing is so much bigger than any inconvenience we could experience! I must add a scripture here that was crucial to my being a better wife: "...whatever is true, whatever is honorable, whatever is right, whatever is pure, whatever is lovely, whatever is of good repute, if there is any excellence or if anything worthy of praise, dwell on these things." Philippians 4:8. Whenever I was upset with Larry, I learned to apply this verse and always concentrate on all his good qualities instead of any shortcomings.

Healing Begins

While at Ft. Bragg, God was also doing a work in me regarding the abortion that I had in 1970. As I mentioned earlier, we were trying to get pregnant. Well, one year went by. Then two years became three years, and still no pregnancy. In 1973, I found out two things. The first thing, I learned from Georgianna while talking with her about her pregnancy. I mentioned to her that I had been pregnant too, but had an abortion. Being a nurse, she asked me how far along I was at the time. I told her that I was ten weeks pregnant at the time of the abortion. She then asked me very gently if I knew that my baby was completely formed at that time. It already had finger nails and toe nails and all it had left to do was grow. That was when I realized that I hadn't ended a pregnancy or removed tissue from my body, I had actually killed my baby. I had always felt something was wrong with abortion, and now I had to go through a healing process with God. I had read the Bible daily since I was born again, including the whole New Testament during the first six months. I knew how much God loved me. I knew He had forgiven me of ALL my sin, including the abortion. I had been washed clean!

But I needed to go through this all again with God, because the guilt and the shame were overwhelming as they are for many women who have had abortions. After receiving my healing, I told God that I felt guilty for not feeling guilty any more. I finally heard Him say to me, "Averie, when I died on the cross, I took your guilt upon Myself! You do not need to carry it any more. Guilt is debilitating. I don't want you to carry it. Regret - yes. You can regret the abortion because that means you would do it differently next time, but let the guilt go!" What wonderful joy and freedom came when I finally let it all go! Thank you, Jesus! You are so awesome!

The second thing Larry and I learned in 1973, after we finally went to the doctor for infertility testing. Following several procedures, it was discovered that a mild infection from the abortion had caused a blockage in my Fallopian tubes. I underwent surgery in January of 1975 at the University of Michigan Medical Center to correct the problem.

Two more years went by. During Christmas weekend 1976, I began having some slight bleeding and moments of intense pain that would come and go. Two days after Christmas, our belongings were packed by the movers because Larry's military commitment was up on December 31, and we were moving to Dayton, Ohio. That night we were staying in a friend's quarters and I awoke in such horrible pain that I could not sit up. Larry turned the light on to see his wife looking as white as the sheets. He rushed me to the hospital where my blood pressure was discovered to be 60/40 and dropping. Emergency surgery was performed, and my right tube and ovary were removed. I had experienced an ectopic pregnancy due to scar tissue from the abortion and previous surgery. The Fallopian tube had burst as the baby grew too large for it to contain. I would have bled to death had Larry not responded so quickly to the situation.

The awesome thing about this experience happened after I woke up while being rolled down the hall after the surgery. I heard the doctor's voice (not able to open my eyes yet) and asked him what had happened. You need to understand that a year earlier, when I first learned what an ectopic pregnancy is from a friend whose doctor thought she might have one (it turned out she did not have one), I told God that that was the one thing I could never go through since we had been trying to get pregnant for so long. The doctor told me what they had done, and I began thinking about it being harder for me to get pregnant now. Immediately, I saw a vision of 2 roads in front of me. The one on the right was dark and on it I saw sadness, anger, depression, pain, bitterness, self-pity and grief. The road on the left was all lit up and Jesus was standing on it, smiling, with His hand held out to me. He said, "All you need is me and you can do anything." I looked at Him and said "OK" and then I took His hand. I was instantaneously filled with an incredible joy that I cannot explain to this day. This joy was a wonderful supernatural joy that stayed with me for three months.

Two hours later, when the nurse was taking me to my 30-bed ward from recovery and getting me into my bed, she told me that she had never seen anyone so happy who had just had major surgery and almost died. Of course, I was not happy about what had happened to me, but she could see this divine joy. Even Mom could not believe how wonderful I looked when she arrived to drive me to Dayton a few days later. Larry had already left to meet our moving van, and I was not able to drive yet, so she flew down from Michigan and drove me in our car to our new house. God is so good! Nothing could ever make me doubt His existence or His love when I remember this special time. Jesus IS ENOUGH in any and every circumstance! To avoid another ectopic pregnancy and possible death, I had a third major surgery to repair my remaining tube six months later in Dayton. That was in 1977 and I have never become pregnant again, but God has been enough to sustain my joy!

One of the things I remember about that night in the hospital was being taken from room to room for x-rays, tests etc. on my rolling bed. Every time I came out Larry was there and I asked him if he had called Lou yet (the AG chaplain's wife). I wanted her and the other ladies in the Bible study to be praying for me, but Larry was embarrassed to call them at 3:00 in the morning. He finally did call her, and they all prayed for me.

More Blessings

We moved to new quarters our last year in the army *(photo pg 49)*. It had 3 bedrooms, 2 baths and a fireplace. I loved it! A special memory there that I will never forget is when Alma, another 2LT's wife, was over. I'd been sharing what I was learning about being a Christian wife with her for many months. When I went into the kitchen to get us something to drink, she said to me, "You know, Averie, I don't even think of you as being white." You see, Alma was African-American and had been raised in Mississippi. Surprised, I turned around and asked, "Why, Alma? Is it bad to be white?" She responded, "Oh yes, there is nothing worse than a white person." Wow! How awful to grow up being treated so badly by a group of people that you feel that way. She paid me a high honor by making that statement.

> "In everything, therefore,
> treat people the same way you want them to treat you,..."
> *Matthew 7:12a*

I began allowing God to use me as a witness here at Ft. Bragg and had the privilege of leading some to the Lord, like Sandy Von Koenel. She was the wife of a captain that was a Rhodes Scholar. She was having a hard time getting pregnant, and was quite depressed one night when the guys were in the field. I drove out to her home and prayed for her, which touched her deeply. She called the next day and wanted to come over to talk. I knew something special was going to happen. When she arrived, she told me she wanted to be like me! What a perfect opportunity! I told her it wasn't me, it was Jesus that was in me. He loved her and she could have him too. After more discussion, we prayed there in the living room of our army quarters. There is nothing more fulfilling or rewarding than leading someone to the Lord!

Shortly before we left for Dayton, our church challenged us to give the 90% to the Lord and keep the 10% for one week. Larry and I prayed and felt we should do it. Well, after signing our contract on our new house in Dayton, the price was lowered by $3,000 and we were given a free car! You cannot out-give God!

Chapter VI

To Dayton

Our army days over, we arrived in Dayton, Ohio on January 3, 1977. We had purchased our first home, and I remember being so nervous while signing the papers because we would have a huge house payment of $315 a month that included property taxes and insurance. If only mortgage payments were that low today!

I soon met Lorraine Baeder at a Bible study that a neighbor told me about. She became a very close friend and a big influence on my spiritual life. She had attended a very strict Baptist church that believed if you spoke in tongues you were of the devil. I didn't know this, and freely shared with Lorraine many special experiences I had with the Lord, including the following...

It was January 1976 when I saw Dad having heart problems in my spirit, and became very burdened about my parents' salvation. It was so heavy, I felt like I could hardly stand up. Larry had gone to Panama for the Jungle Warfare School, and I was going to a revival service at a Pentecostal Holiness church with a friend that night. She prayed with me in the car that God would give me an answer before the service was over. I needed to know if I should fly to my parents and talk to them. There was a time of worship, followed by a prayer. At the end of the prayer there was a short silence, when God spoke to me and said, "This is for you." Then came a message in tongues, followed by the interpretation: "Do not be burdened for the loved ones you have been praying for any longer. I have already sent angels to minister to them and your whole family will be saved." I began to sob. I was humbled that God would answer me so clearly. In May, I was home for Rudy's wedding, and Mom and Dad were both open to talk about spiritual things for the first time since I was born again.

Then, in August, I came home while Larry was in the field, and found out that Dad had been scheduled for open heart surgery! I was able to lead Dad in a salvation prayer the next evening! Thank you, Lord! I didn't know what to tell him next and prayed for God to send someone to help Dad. A few days later, Dad was in the hospital for the surgery, and an older man carrying a Bible walked into his room. He had worked for Dad 35 years earlier and was now a Baptist minister. After hearing Dad was in the hospital, he came to see him and shared about salvation. Dad told him that he had just prayed that prayer with me a few days ago, so he opened his Bible and took it from there. He shared things I just didn't know how to explain yet. It was great!

Lorraine eventually told me what she had been taught, but also that she felt God's presence whenever I shared these spiritual things with her. She knew that I really knew God, and eventually, she and her husband Bill were both baptized in the Holy Spirit. Because of Lorraine's beliefs, I read through the whole New Testament again so that I could know biblically why I believed what I believed. It was a very beneficial exercise that God used to enable me to share these truths with many others in my future. Lorraine was very wise and I learned a lot from her during those years about raising children and serving your husband. I had great admiration and love for her. Larry and I spent a lot of good times with Bill and Lorraine as couples. Bill had a quick wit and Larry loved the bantering back and forth. Lorraine joined in too, but I never did. I just couldn't compete.

> "...there is a friend who sticks closer
> than a brother."
>
> *Proverbs 18:24b*

Continuing to Grow in the Lord

Larry and I both grew so much spiritually here in Dayton. We tried several different churches (all different denominations), but fell in love with Kettering Assembly of God about 20 minutes from our house. Pastor Ross was a great preacher, and very wise. During every service for the 2 1/2 years that we lived in Dayton, I received a new revelation of God's Word - mostly from Pastor Ross' sermons. It was incredible! Of course, I was doing my own study at home and reading the word every day. The wonderful thing was that I would feel like God was teaching me something from His word, and then many times Pastor Ross would teach the same thing the next service at church. God was showing me that I didn't have to rely solely on ministers to learn, but that God would teach me Himself if I would stay in His Word and seek Him! I enjoyed the Baptist Bible study that I attended with Lorraine immensely. They were great ladies and they enjoyed my input. It was funny, but God seemed to prepare me ahead of time. So many times, I would have just memorized a certain scripture, and the teacher would reference it that very week in class! The ladies thought I had the whole bible memorized. When it came time for us to move to Michigan, several of the ladies said that the study would not be the same without me. What a kind thing to say! But I missed them too.

One thing that helped me grow spiritually while in Dayton, was memorizing the book of Philippians. This was a life-changing exercise! There are many well-known verses in this book that many memorize, but I was amazed at how God used the seemingly insignificant verses to bless me during the day! I still rely on much of this book to build my faith and to make me more like Him!

While in Dayton, Larry used some of his GI Bill money to rent an airplane for us fly to Jacksonville, Florida to see Tim and Georgianna. When Larry was checking the plane before takeoff, he noticed that the gas gauge was not working (said half full when it was full). He asked about it and was told he would have plenty of gas according to the miles to Jacksonville (and Larry's own calculations.) However, we ran into some thunderstorms that we had to fly around, which used up more gas than planned. When we were over Alma, Georgia, Larry switched the gas tanks from "both" to the "right" tank. About 5 minutes later the plane sputtered and the engine stopped. The right tank was out of gas, which meant there was about five minutes of gas in the left tank. Larry quickly began pulling levers and trying to get the plane started again. Finally, the engine came back on!! He called the Alma tower to ask where the nearest airport was with lights (because it was now dark.) He was told Waycross, which was more than five minutes away. Then, suddenly, Larry started to shout praises to God. I joined him immediately. We shouted, "Praise the Lord!", "Glory to God!" and other praises to God continuously in that airplane for the next twenty minutes as we headed toward Waycross. We landed safely and found a dime taped to the window of an old phone booth on the runway. There was a sign that said if you need gas call this number. We filled the tanks and made it the rest of the way to Jacksonville safely. I believe God got us to that airport supernaturally! He is an awesome God!

"Delight yourself in the LORD;
and He will give you the desires of your heart."
Psalm 37:4

A Big Day

One of the most important things that happened in Dayton, was our son Bill's adoption. Lorraine had used Lutheran Social Services, so we used them as well. There were case studies and classes that we had to complete. But after almost two years, Dick Young interviewed Larry for a job in Grand Rapids, Michigan. It was November, and when we checked with the adoption agency, they said we were #3 on the list and should have our baby by the middle of December. The timing would have been perfect, but as Larry and I prayed, we just could not get a peace about it so Larry turned the offer down. December came and went. Then January and February, and still no baby!

On March 6, Dick Young flew Larry to Michigan for another interview and gave him until Friday to decide. We called the adoption agency and we were still #3 on the list. On Friday, after much prayer all week, Larry called and accepted the offer. What we didn't know was that 2 babies were placed that week and Bill's mom brought him to the agency on Friday. We put our house up for sale on Tuesday and got two offers for full price that night. Then on Wednesday, the agency told us they had a baby for us to pick up on Friday! We were in Michigan 3 weeks later. God's timing is always perfect! Of course, the Friday that we picked up Bill was a huge day in our lives. It was obvious that God had picked out Bill just for us, having his mother wait until the day that we were next on the list to bring him in to the agency! Most babies were born, placed in a foster home for 3 or 4 days, and then placed with the adoptive family. Bill was 2 months and 3 weeks old when he came to us. We picked him up at the agency in downtown Dayton and then took him right over to Lorraine and Bill's for them to see him *(photo pg 49)*. Mom flew in later that afternoon to help me out the first few days with our first baby. It was a wonderful day!

Dayton was a time of growth for Larry too. Even though he worked 7 days a week when he was at GM, he learned so much and really grew as the spiritual leader of our home. We learned about faith, sometimes by trial and error! We had a group of friends that would meet from house to house, taking turns. We would worship and discuss things of the Lord. God really moved and our memories of those days are very special to us.

I was able to lead several people to the Lord during our 2-1/2 years in Dayton. One was Lucy, a "witch" that I met at our adoption class. She said her grandmother was a witch and prayed over her many times for spiritual powers. I had never met anyone who said they were a witch before. It was an interesting experience. Another person was Miss Markhoff. She was an 80-year-old spinster in a wheelchair who needed help. She paid me $2 an hour to drive her to the store, take her out to lunch, pay her bills, clean up her messes when she had accidents and other miscellaneous things around her apartment. She was a tough old lady that could be quite harsh, but I didn't mind. I was so glad that she accepted the Lord before she died! While we lived in Dayton, I saw Larry in the ministry (in my spirit) a couple of times, and asked him if he had thought of becoming a minister. Each time he said, "No way!" I didn't think he would consider it, but I pondered it in my heart.

Neland Ave.
*(with Chip, Mom &
me in the window)*

Hall Street

Mom, Dad ▲
& Me

Hall Street ▶

45

1952-1967

Family
Vacations

High School
Graduation

Far Right:
   Doll Chair

TOP LEFT:
with Grandma & Grandpa Behler
I'm on the left, center row

TOP RIGHT: Camp

MID LEFT:
Mrs. DePew 2nd Grade

MID RIGHT & BOTTOM:
Cheerleading

WEDDING PHOTOS:
Grace Episcopal Church

LOWER RIGHT:
Potter's Pond *(We were baptized just to the right of the bridge)*

TOP: Army Housing
MID-LEFT: Lorraine holding Bill
MID-RIGHT: Introduced as Pastor of Marriage & Family
BOTTOM-LEFT: Family Picture
BOTTOM-RIGHT: with the Wilkerson's at Ft. Bragg, NC

49

TOP LEFT:
Arriving in Gosaba, India

TOP RIGHT:
Praying at symposium

BOTTOM
Speaking to students about
abstinence.

NEXT TWO PAGES: ▶
Letters from students

March 31, 1994

Dear Mrs. Alverson,

How are you? I wanted to thank you for coming to speak to us. I learned alot of things people just don't tell us. One of the things I learned was to wait to have sex after your married. I didn't know that condoms were not 100% safe.

I think a person like you should tell people the consequences that having sex before your married will have an effect later in your life.

I give you lots of respect for telling us your experience in your life. I hope people will listen and learn like I did. Once again, Thank you!

Sincerely,
████████████

3-31-94

Dear Mrs. Alverson,

Yesterday you came to East Kentwood Highschool and talked to my Health class. I really enjoyed your presentation. I'm 15 yrs old and I have a boyfriend who is 17. We have both talked about having sex before. I wasn't to sure about it. Hearing you speak yesterday about what can happen when you have sex, Kinda scared me!

Last night my boyfriend came over and we talked & showed him the paper you gave us and the chastity card. Last night we talked for a long time about chastity. I signed the card and he was my witness.

Thanks for coming & enjoyed listening to you speak.
Thanks again,
████████████

Dear Mrs. Alverson,   3-31-94

I really, truly enjoyed your presentation on sex. Many speakers that I listen to are boring and they can't really relate to us as teenagers. By sharing your own experiences, we could understand what you went through. I learned that the safest way to avoid diseases and pregnancy is to abstain from sex and other sexual actions. I want you to know that we appreciate you and that you really did make a difference.

Sincerely,
████████████

51

March 31, 1994

Dear Mrs. Alverson,

My name is Shari Clark and I am fifteen years old. I was very glad that an experienced adult could come talk about this subject.

You are one of the very few adults who still widely and openly have the courage to tell kids they can wait. As a Christian I fully believe in waiting til I am married. A lot of teenagers have sex but are so naive about the physical and emotional consequences. I feel your approach is very pure and from the heart. Many points need to hear your speech too.

* (During your speech I found that many of the student who were and are sexually active agreed with you or had some kind of effect brought on them.) * (I hope and think you should council) teenagers one-on-one. I liked your talk, it was not overwhelming but straight to the point. Keep speaking.

Sincerely,

52

CONGRATULATIONS!

WHAT AN AWESOME JOB, MOM

WE'RE PROUD OF YOU, AVE!

THANKS FOR YOUR FAITHFULNESS TO THE CALL OF GOD ON YOUR LIFE. YOU'RE THE GREATEST!

love, **B**uckshot **B**ill **B**etsy

TOP: (left) Larry's card   **(right)** Flyer
BOTTOM: With Governor Engler at signing of the Informed Consent bill

THE GRAND RAPIDS PRESS

BORN AGAIN

Post-abortion group helps heal emotional scars

By Leigh Ann Eagleston
The Grand Rapids Press

L ynn Braybrook Roelofs named her second daughter when she saw her image on the ultrasound in the 10th week of her pregnancy.

That action and the name itself – Hope – say a lot about the 38-year-old Hudsonville woman's outlook on children and life these days.

But during her first marriage 15 years ago, Roelofs was so afraid of becoming pregnant she could not consummate the union. And though her depression was severe, she could not cry for 17 years.

Today, Roelofs attributes both the fear and depression to her first pregnancy at 17 and the way it ended – in abortion.

It was not until many years later, after being told by a counselor that she needed to "grieve the abortion," that Roelofs says she came to terms with her pain.

"I cried out to God and asked his forgiveness ... and I felt an overwhelming peace," she said.

Now a strong proponent of the pro-life movement, Roelofs and Averie Alverson of Wyoming are seeking to pass on their peace through support groups run by post-abortive women for post-abortive women. They call it Mourning Joy Ministries.

Other groups also offer help in different ways. Post-abortion counseling is available through Project Rachel in the Catholic Diocese of Grand Rapids, said coordinator Pat Ryan. The service

> **❝** *I cried out to God and asked his forgiveness... and I felt an overwhelming peace.* **❞**
>
> LYNN ROELOFS

see GROUP, B2

NEXT PAGE TOP LEFT: Washington, D.C.
MIDDLE: Installation at Trinity
RIGHT: 1st Assembly Farewell
BOTTOM: Bible Study Group

TOP: Preaching in the Philippines
BOTTOM: Bamboo Church

OPENING DISNEYWORLD WITH MICKEY MOUSE!

TOP: With Pastor Wayne & Kathy Benson
BOTTOM: On Mackinac Island with Ron & Vicky Smit

 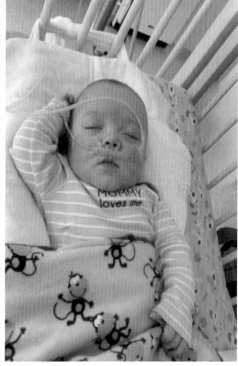

TOP: With Granddaughter Kaylee **BOTTOM:** Gina & me (left)
Grandson Jaxon (right)

Chapter VII
The 1980's

The 80's began with the death of my dad on March 1. I got a call from Mom on Wednesday to tell me that he was in the hospital and things did not look good. I flew to Brownsville, Texas where they had just moved into their new winter home. By the time I arrived at the hospital on Thursday night, Dad was already in a coma. I had prayed on the trip down and kept hearing in my spirit that he was going to live. Chip arrived Friday. Then on Saturday morning, I was making the bed when I heard it again - only this time it was, "He is going to live forever." I stood up straight and said "No!" I knew that it meant he was going to die, but that he was saved. When I went into the kitchen five minutes later where Mom and Chip were, the phone rang. It was the doctor calling to tell Mom that Dad had died five minutes earlier. I was so thankful that God had prepared me and let me know he would be in heaven. I was shocked when my very first response to the news in just a flash of a second was envy - I wanted to be where he was, I wanted to know what he knew, and I wanted to see what he was seeing! Then in the next second came the loss and grief. He was a great dad and has been sorely missed all these years. The church was packed (with over 700) for the funeral, and over 1,000 came to the funeral home. Thank you, Lord, for giving him to us!

In 1982, we adopted Betsy through the Highlands Child Placement Agency. She also was 2 months and 3 weeks old when we picked her up in Kansas City. We took Bill with us, and when he first saw her, he looked at her with a puzzled look and asked, "Does she talk?" We said not yet. He said, "Can she walk?" We told him no, and he just walked away, disappointed that he couldn't do much with her. She was so cute with her red hair, which later became strawberry blonde.

When Betsy was four years old, I heard a thump in her bedroom where she was taking a nap, and found her on the floor having a seizure. I picked her up and ran to the kitchen screaming for Vicky Zudweg who was in the garage. By the time Vicky arrived, she was coming around and seemed fine. I called the doctor but he didn't seem concerned. Everyone thought she was just waking up from her nap a little groggy. A year later, it happened again while Larry was home getting ready for work. When he got to me he took Betsy from me and she stopped breathing, her heart stopped beating, her eyes dilated and her bladder emptied. He took her to the living room to do CPR while I called 911. Larry revived her before the paramedics arrived and this time the doctor wanted us to take her to the hospital for testing. After many tests, they discovered she had abnormal brain waves while sleeping and waking up, but made no definitive diagnosis at that time.

I was afraid to ever leave her alone - what would have happened had I not been with her. After three days of feeling nauseated and like I was in a dream, I told the Lord I could not live like this. I gave her to Him and asked Him to take care of her. After all, she was His anyway and just loaned to me for a while. I felt such peace and relief! She continued to have seizures until she was almost nine when she had her worst one yet. We went back to the neurologist who diagnosed her with epilepsy. He asked if I wanted to put her on anti-seizure medication since her seizures would probably be more often and violent now that she was starting puberty. I decided not to because the doctor said the medicine would affect her scholastics, and Betsy was already in special education classes. The next Sunday we took Betsy to the altar and had her anointed with oil and prayed for again. She never had another seizure after that. I am so glad we didn't put her on the medication or we would not have known God had healed her! He has been so faithful to us in so many ways.

"The LORD has done great things for us; We are glad."

Psalm 126:3

In 1980, I had now known the Lord for eight years. He was teaching me so many things and changing me in so many ways. One of the first things He had to change in me was my low self-esteem. Over the years, people had blessed me and encouraged me, but God also had to allow the other side as well. I had many hurtful things happen to me and said to me, that were sometimes intentional and many times unintentional. An example was Dad's funeral. So many people paid their respects, but only one person from our church - John Penning, who knew of Dad from his business, came to the visitation or the funeral. I was very hurt, and Larry and I even went to another church the next Sunday. It was nice, but we knew God had called us to 1st Assembly, and Larry had been asked to serve as one of the first elders that same week. God told me not to be hurt by this. He said that I didn't know all that was going on and that I was very much loved by Him. He wanted me to always go to Him when I was hurt and to let the hurt go. He had already shown me that low self-esteem was nothing more than self-centeredness and pride – always speculating what people are thinking about you. He wanted me to focus on others and not myself. We returned to 1st Assembly, and two weeks later I ran into Pastor Benson in the hall. He asked how I was doing and asked where the funeral had been held. I told him it was at Grace Episcopal Church at Hall and Plymouth. His faced turned white and he looked shocked. He had been out of town when Dad died and the young youth pastor had talked to Larry. He had not asked Larry the right questions and just assumed that the funeral was in Texas, and that is what the church was told. No one had come because they didn't know the funeral was in Grand Rapids!

2 Timothy 2:23 says "But refuse foolish and ignorant speculations..." When God made this verse real to me, I realized how many times I would speculate people's motives and why they did or said things. Most of the time, we are probably wrong - just like in the case of Dad's

funeral. What happened did not mean what I thought it did. Applying this verse to my life has been such a blessing! My love for the Lord and my relationship with him has just grown so much more with every difficult situation I have had to face. I cannot imagine what my life would have been like without His life-giving Word to guide me and change me!

"Consider it all joy, my brethren,
when you encounter various trials,
knowing that the testing of your faith produces
endurance."
James 1:2-3

An exciting thing happened soon after arriving in Grand Rapids. Before we left Dayton, I had tried to reach a large vase on a high shelf and dropped it on my left big toe. My toenail turned black and eventually fell off. My toe looked pretty gross and mangled without the nail on it. After a year and a half with no toenail, I asked my doctor about it. He told me that I had killed the root of the nail and would never have a nail on that toe again. The next spring, I was getting dressed and looked at my ugly toe and lamented to the Lord that my toe was going to look so ugly when I wore my sandals. I didn't ask Him to heal it, but two weeks later when I was getting dressed, I looked at my foot and saw a beautiful complete toenail on my big toe! God had healed it for me. What a blessing!

The Call to the Ministry

Every year Larry had an elder lunch with Pastor Benson. In 1982, he asked Larry if he had ever considered the ministry, fulltime. Larry told him no and forgot about it. Then at their meeting in February of 1983, Pastor Benson asked him the same question and received the same answer, but asked Larry if he would pray about it this time. Larry agreed to pray about it, and just a half mile up the road after he left the restaurant, Larry knew in his spirit that God wanted him to go in the ministry! This was not what he wanted to hear. He had no desire to go into the ministry! For two weeks, he argued with God. He would go to work and felt this is where he belonged, but then would toss and turn all night long arguing with God about it. By the morning, he would say, "Yes" to God, but by the next evening he changed his mind again. After two weeks of this, he finally went to the altar at the church service and submitted to God's call on his life. It was terrifying for Larry because he felt totally unqualified for this job. I had total peace about this because God had shown me in my spirit many years ago that this was going to happen. I knew it was His will for us! Larry gave a nine-month notice at work. In September, they announced to 1st Assembly that Larry was coming on staff as the new Marriage and Family Pastor *(photo pg 49)*, and he was installed on January 1, 1984. What an honor and privilege to serve God in this way.

Since our pay was drastically cut, we sold our home and bought a less expensive one closer to the church, went from two cars to one, and changed our budget - we began using the "envelope system" which worked great for us. Because our children were small, we never considered that I would go to work and not be home with them. Of course, this was a huge transition for us, but it has been a wonderful adventure!

I remember telling God how honored we were to serve Him like this, and that I didn't even mind giving up the traveling that we had begun to enjoy because of the business trips we had been able to take. I think God must have chuckled at that. I had no idea that the ministry would send us on many fantastic mission trips around the world that we would have never been able to take otherwise. We have been to El Salvador, Argentina, many countries in Europe, India, Korea, China, The Congo, The Philippines, Jamaica, Togo, Ghana, Ethiopia and Mexico. As I have said before, you just cannot out-give God. Whatever we think we give up for Him, He somehow returns a bigger blessing to us. It took Larry a few months to get used to the change of occupation, but God is faithful, and began to give him a pastor's heart. He completed 72 hours of course work and was credentialed with the

Assemblies of God and later ordained in 1988. We enjoyed the Marriage and Family ministry, but less than two years later, Larry would give that ministry to Pastor Klingenberg, and take on the administration of the church as well as missions, men's and singles ministries. He eventually became the senior associate (Pastor Benson's right-hand man). What a privilege to be mentored in the ministry by Pastor Benson at 1st Assembly.

Love Never Fails...1 Cor. 13:8

I had been born again for about 10 years now, and I was noticing something as I read through the Bible each year. God's love is so wonderful and unconditional. He is so merciful and gives grace to us constantly. But I was a "rule-obeyer". Unfortunately, when you are a "rule-obeyer", it is very easy to look at others that we think are not obeying whatever rules we think should be obeyed, and we can become judgmental or just not loving like God is. I told God that I didn't love people the way He did in His Word. I asked Him to help me see people and love people like He did. You see, each one of us looks at others through our own perspective, based on our own experiences. We just don't look at individual people like God does. We cannot love them unless God helps us see them like He does.

Well, it has been an amazing journey since I began praying that prayer. God began to stop me in the middle of my observations and thoughts of people and show me what he thought when He looked at them. Let me give you a few examples. One day I was at Rogers Department Store, which was a wonderful store that gave impeccable service. That day was very busy! I was waited on by a lady I had never seen before, and she was in a very bad mood. She was being quite rude to me and the other clerks were looking at her like "What are you doing?!" But suddenly I saw the Lord's concern for her and He told me not to take it personally. I should pray for her because I did not know what was going on in her life that day and she did not need more stress from me. Of course, that changed everything and I did pray for her.

One Sunday during worship at church, I was noticing one of the ladies who had come to the altar to worship as she often did. She was dressed in one of her usual cowgirl dresses with lots of fringe on the sleeves and bottom. I started to think to myself, "Why does she always wear those strange clothes?" Immediately, I felt the Lord enjoying watching her enjoy her cowgirl clothes! Why should I care what she wore? She is the one who should enjoy what she is wearing, and I can wear what I enjoy wearing!

The most powerful experience came one day when I was folding clothes in our family room. I sat down and flipped through the channels and settled on a biography of Cindy Lauper. I had heard of her but did not know anything about her. In the first clip, she was singing a pretty song, had blonde hair and her voice sounded like an angel's to me. But in subsequent clips, she was wearing unusual and outstanding clothes (you couldn't miss noticing her in a crowd), and her hair was green or purple or bright red and kind of wild. I thought, "You are so pretty and have such a pretty voice, why do you ruin it with your hair and clothes?" Suddenly, I felt this huge, incredible love that God has for her and tears filled my eyes. It was an overwhelming love! Then I felt God's pleasure in watching her use the creativity that He had put within her. I certainly hadn't thought of it as creativity. Then He said to me, "Averie, I don't care what color her hair is. Why do you?" I began crying and asked God to forgive me. I was so glad that He loves me with the same incredible love with which He loves her (and every other person on this earth). We need to give each other space to be who we are, and not expect them to think and be like us. What a boring world that would be. Many of the things we think are important, in fact, matter very little.

God's Economy

I have already mentioned some of the previous times that God has blessed us financially because we decided to be faithful with the tithe that belongs to Him. The 80's began and ended with a couple more great stories of God's provision. The first one was in November, when our church was going to televise our Singing Christmas Tree production. It was going to cost $30,000. They told us about it and took an offering to pay for it during an evening service. Larry and I had been saving money to buy a piece of carpeting to put on our family room floor. It was a brick floor and very hard on Bill's knees since he was still crawling. We had $300 saved so far and decided to give that toward the production. As I put the check in the offering, I prayed that God would multiply it 100-fold. I later realized that 100 times 300 was 30,000. Well, $30,000 came in that night. Then a couple of weeks later, we received $3,000 totally out of the blue from an unexpected source! The church had received 100-fold and we had received 10-fold! Obviously, we were able to purchase the much-needed carpet for our home.

Then in October of 1988, our church was receiving faith promises for our new 5,000 seat sanctuary that we were going to build. When Larry and I prayed separately about it, we each thought we heard the Lord say $20,000! That was a huge amount for us to pay over the three years of the faith promise on an associate pastor's salary, but since we both heard the same amount, we decided we should be obedient. When I sat down and divided the amount by the number of paychecks the next three years, we were about $10 a paycheck short of what we needed if no emergencies happened (like flat tires or broken refrigerators, etc.) Another problem was our property taxes coming up in February. We had nothing saved to pay them so I began praying for God to supply our need as we were faithful to our faith promise. We also cancelled a vacation to Disney World that we had put a deposit down on since we would not have the money to go in the spring.

A week before our taxes were due, we still had no money for the bill. We received our MBA (our retirement) statement in the mail and it always just had the amount the church had put in and then the total in the account. This time, however, there was another number under "Personal Savings Account." I called to find out what this was and was told it was our savings account that we could use any time by calling and requesting a check. Our tax bill was $907 and there was $913 in the savings account. We believe that God put that money in our account, because we didn't even know we had it. The check arrived just in time to pay the bill! That week we also got a call from Mom saying she was sending us 4 airplane tickets to fly to Texas for spring break and we had a wonderful free vacation! What an awesome God we serve! By the way, we were able to complete our faith promise during the rest of the three years with no problem. One more note: You will enjoy reading the story near the end of the book about how God restored our trip to Disney World.

> "Give, and it will be given to you.
> They will pour into your lap a good measure —
> pressed down, shaken together, and running over.
> For by your standard of measure
> it will be measured to you in return."
> *Luke 6:38*

Learning Patience and Trust

After Larry submitted to God and agreed to go into full-time ministry, we decided to prepare. It was the end of March of 1983 and he would be coming on staff January 1, 1984. The first thing we did was to put our house up for sale, so we could purchase a less expensive home closer to the church. Things seemed to be going smoothly when a nice couple with two darling little girls bought our house just a few weeks later.

We then purchased our new home and moved in the end of June. The family moved into our home the middle of July, paying rent for the two weeks in July, with the closing scheduled for the end of August. The August rent check never arrived, and they did not show up for the closing. That night we were watching the 11 pm news and there was the husband…the front and side view photos, with numbers underneath… AND, he had a different name! Our neighbors told us that right after they moved in, they put up a 6 foot fence with a gate across the driveway. Cars would back in and come out with different license plates. (They could see them from their upstairs windows.)

Well, we had to hire a lawyer and go to court to evict them. All of this was not completed until the end of September when the peak real estate market was winding down. We were making two house payments and paying for lawyers when we hoped to be saving money to help with the transition. When we got our house back, there was a black mist of paint on some of the walls and doors. The family had hired Mayflower Van Lines to move them, but after they had packed their belongings, they spray painted over the Mayflower logos and used another company to do the move without paying Mayflower for the packing. Fortunately, Mayflower found out and put a hold on the delivery until they were paid. We saw in the news a couple months later that the man had been arrested for forging letters on White House stationery.

Our house finally did sell on December 23, 1983 with the closing set for the end of January. Then, five days before the closing, the police called me out of the Sunday evening church service because our neighbors had called them after noticing a waterfall coming out of our upstairs bathroom window. The pipes had frozen and burst and all three floors of the house were flooded. Fortunately, the closing took place as planned when the buyers realized that our insurance company would pay for the repairs and that they could pick out whatever they wanted for the renovation.

We entered the ministry on January 1 with our savings depleted, knowing that God is our provider. Learning patience and trust as we waited and watched God meet our every need just in time was a valuable lesson for our future calling. God is so good!

"..Go into all the world..."
Mark 16:15

One of the great adventures of my walk with God has been taking missions trips. Larry and I had the incredible opportunity to take our first trip to Calcutta Mission of Mercy that was established by Assembly of God missionary, Mark Buntain. He was a mighty man of God and we could sense God's presence whenever we were with him. We first flew to Seoul, South Korea where we spent a couple of days visiting the largest church in the world - Yoido Church that had 700,000 members at the time. We attended a service in the 25,000-seat auditorium. We sat in the balcony where they had earphones to hear the service in several different languages. They have several services on Sunday and many members meeting at other locations around the city. We also went to prayer mountain - we have never seen such a praying people before! It was very humbling.

We flew from Seoul to Hong Kong to Bangkok, and then Calcutta. There is no other place on earth quite like Calcutta. On our last day there, the cab driver told us what a National Geographic photographer that he was driving said, "Calcutta is a vision of the end of man!" I totally agreed with his comment. Larry preached at several services in Calcutta and other outlying villages and I spoke to the women's group. We visited the schools that educated 20,000 children from the slums. We went to the feeding programs where 25,000 people were fed every day. We toured the beautiful hospital and nursing school that Mark had built.

Our favorite part of the trip was a two-and-a-half-hour drive to the Ganges River, where we caught a sampan. We then traveled down the river a few hours to the village of Gosaba. First Assembly had provided the funds to build a church building there, and they wanted to meet us and have Larry preach. The people greeted us, put leis on us and touched our feet when we arrived. Mark let us know ahead of time that this was a customary way of honoring the clergy *(photo pg 50)*. I was the first white woman to be there in over 50 years. We ate lunch and after the service went further up the river to the Bengal tiger reserve to spend the night. To experience how people live in so much of the world makes you realize very quickly how blessed we are to live in the U.S.! The pastor of that little church had two college degrees and lived in a mud two-room house with one piece of furniture - a double bed that he and his wife and two teenage daughters slept in. They cooked outside over an open fire. I don't think we were ever the same after returning from this trip!

We took a trip to Europe in June 1988. We went with a construction team to help build a church in Brussels. Larry and I traveled to the Netherlands for a night to visit Tim and Georgianna who were stationed there. We then went to England where Larry spoke to a church board. From there we went to Paris where Larry preached at the Tuesday night service with missionary Henry Linderman. Our next stop was Augsburg, Germany where Larry preached to the U.S. troops stationed there with missionary Bob Way. It was an awesome trip and I was thrilled to be able to see where Larry lived in Germany when he was 10-12 years old, while his dad was stationed there.

Lord, Am I Going Crazy?

I had held a Bible Study in my home for a few ladies who were new believers. Eventually we moved it to the church where more ladies attended. God was developing my speaking abilities for things in the future that I knew nothing about. In 1987, I went through three months of severe depression during which I did not want to leave my bedroom or see anyone. I had two small children to take care, so I had to get up and do my best. It was scary because there was no reason for me to be depressed. However, I felt so awful, and my strong will and self-control didn't seem to help me get out of it. I felt like a failure as a wife, mother, friend, Christian, pastor's wife, and that everyone would be better off if I were not there. I knew the Word and that this was a lie, but it didn't change how I felt. It was like I was in the middle of the sea at midnight during a rain storm. The only rope I had to hang on to so I wouldn't drown was the Word of God. I asked God if I should counsel with Pastor Benson or check into a mental hospital. I heard God saying to depend upon Him and that there was light at the end of this darkness. This went on for three months, and while listening to a tape about Jesus being the only one who can heal a broken spirit based on Proverbs 18:14 "The spirit of a man can endure his sickness, but as for a broken spirit who can bear?" I felt God healing my spirit as I listened. When the tape was done, I asked God if He was healing me, and walked to the mailbox which had a card for me. I opened the card as I walked down the sidewalk to meet Betsy at the school bus stop. The card said, "Jesus, the only one who can heal you, body, soul, and spirit." The gal who sent the card had bought it a month before and heard God tell her to mail it to me two days earlier!!! She had no idea what I was going through, but God used her to bless me.

> "Be strong and let your heart take courage,
> all you who hope in the Lord."
>
> *Psalm 31:24*

The next year, the church was having a women's symposium, and they asked me to be the main speaker. I told them I would be happy to do that and that my topic would be "Lord, Am I Going Crazy?" I had just been through feeling like this and knew there must be others out there facing the same thing. After I was done speaking, many came to the altar to pray or be prayed for *(photo pg 50)*. I prayed for one lady that asked me to pray for her, and in the middle of my prayer, I asked God to help her not be lazy. I was shocked to hear that come out of my mouth and was embarrassed that I said that. Later, I was in the narthex and almost everyone was gone when I felt a tap on my shoulder. It was that same lady, and she thanked me for praying for her, especially that part about not being lazy! God always knows what He is doing - we just need to listen and obey! God has used that difficult three months to enable me to minister to many people over the years. It gave me more mercy and compassion for those who need to be carried for a little while until their healing comes. A funny thing happened because of this conference. My mom was getting her nails done, and it turned out that her nail lady had been at the conference and was telling Mom about it. Mom told her that she was my mom. Well, all my life I had been known as Bev and Jack

Behler's daughter, but this lady said "You are Averie Alverson's mom?! You are really Averie Alverson's mom?" We had a good laugh at that.

"A friend loves at all times..."

Proverbs 17:17a

When Larry went into the ministry, we moved to a house in Grandville, and so did our friends, Bill and Lorraine. In 1988, my relationship with Lorraine changed, much to my dismay. She was still a very precious friend to me. However, she said some very hurtful things to me, and I just could not figure out where it was coming from. As I prayed about it, God told me the only thing He expected of me was that I love her. Whenever someone did or said something hurtful to me, I always took it to the Lord, and this was always His response to me. Love them. Finally, I didn't need to ask Him what to do anymore. The answer is always to love them - friend or enemy - love them. "Never pay back evil for evil to anyone. Respect what is right in the sight of all men.... Do not be overcome by evil, but overcome evil with good." Romans 12:17, 21. It was a huge loss to me, but I did not know all that was going on in her life at the time. Bill eventually left her and the kids and moved to California for a new lifestyle. I would pray for her and occasionally I would see her, or stop by for a visit, but we saw very little of each other. Years later, in 2006, I ran into her at a wedding. She told me she and Rick (her new husband) were moving to Tulsa, Oklahoma. As I was leaving the reception, I saw her and hugged her and said, "I love you, Lorraine." She looked at me and said, "You are a good woman, Averie Alverson, and you have been a good friend." I cannot tell you the healing that I felt at that moment. I did not expect to hear anything like that until I reached heaven, but after 18 years, these words were music to my ears.

Chapter VIII

The 1990's

Post-Abortion Ministry is Born

The 90's brought many new things into our lives. One huge thing was the fulfillment of what God told me 18 years earlier - that I would be speaking about my abortion experience some day. I had been volunteering at a crisis pregnancy center for a few years when a call came from Right to Life of Michigan. They were looking for women who had experienced an abortion and would be willing to testify in Lansing before the House and Senate committees considering Informed Consent Legislation.

> "...I have set before you life and death,
> the blessing and the curse.
> So choose life in order that you may live,
> you and your descendants,"
>
> *Deut. 30:19*

They were tired of the pro-life and the pro-abortion group's rhetoric, and wanted to hear from women who had experienced abortion - what did they think about this legislation? I went to Lansing several times to testify along with 16 other women from across the state. Every one of them said the legislation was good and they wished they had received the information before they made their choice. I was invited to be at the signing of the bill into law with Governor Engler *(photo pg 53)*.

Because of this, Pastor Benson asked me to give my testimony in front of our church, which led to several women, including an elder's wife, coming to me about their own abortions. Vicky Smit and I began leading support groups for these women and saw miracles take place before our eyes. The ladies would come with no life in their eyes, depressed and very sad and looking down. In eight short weeks, their countenance would be totally transformed with a smile on their faces and they would be set free. It was like seeing Psalm 3:3 come to life before my eyes – He's the glory and the lifter of my head. One lady had been in therapy for twelve years and had tried to kill herself five times. She began to be set free the very first week. Another had been having panic attacks for nine years and unable to drive her car. We had someone bring her to the group, but by the third week she could drive herself. During the 7th week of one group, one of the ladies said, "Look at us! Just look at us laughing! Who would have thought a few weeks ago that we would be here laughing like this!" What a rewarding experience.

Mourning Joy Ministries

While testifying in Lansing, I met Lynn Roelofs. When we discovered that we were both holding support groups and using the same materials for the groups, we were led to establish Mourning Joy Ministries (MJM) as a 501c3 tax exempt ministry. During the next several years, MJM could help hundreds of men and women in the Grand Rapids area to be set free from the shame and guilt of abortions in their past. People respond in their own way to abortion. Many do not even know that some of the symptoms in their lives are a direct result from an abortion in their past. One of our ladies was sent to us by her therapist, because she had been helping her for years and not getting anywhere. She saw our ad in the paper and told her to try us. She is the lady who was having panic attacks. Only Jesus can truly set someone free from the guilt and shame. Many of the ladies that completed the group became our new leaders. They were so excited about what God had done for them that they wanted to help others be set free too. At the end of each group, we had a memorial service. Since you have an abortion because you don't want to acknowledge the baby's existence, the memorial service acknowledges the baby and brings a special closure to the healing process. We always had a cake with the babies' names on it with some refreshments. When I first heard of doing this, I didn't like the idea, but the Lord showed Vicky and me how important it is for the men and women who go through the group.

The *Grand Rapids Press* sent a reporter to interview Lynn and me. We had no idea why he wanted to do this story or how he would portray MJM, since abortion is such a controversial subject. He did a great job and did a very accurate story. He even commissioned an artist to do the drawing for the story. God was truly blessing us as we tried to minister His love and healing to the men and women of Grand Rapids. *(article pg 54)*

Teaching Abstinence in Schools

After a couple of years with MJM, different people and organizations were hearing about MJM and Lynn and me. We began to get many opportunities to speak in churches, public and private schools and church youth groups. At first it was just about the abortion issue, but one day I received a call from Kentwood public schools with a request to speak to their students about abstinence *(photo pg 50)*. I had never done that before, but had often thought, "If only someone had come to our high school and talked about why it is good to wait to have sex until marriage, it might have spared me a lot of difficulties in my life." After praying about it, I knew that God wanted me to do this. I must admit, however, that it absolutely terrified me. Why would these kids want to listen to a lady in her 40's? I knew they would probably just laugh at me like I was laughed at in my own high school. I went to Right to Life and got a lot of information about abstinence from them. I organized it all and laid it out across my desk and asked God what I was supposed to say to these kids. God showed me how this was not going to be a "negative, sex is bad, depriving yourself" lecture. It was going to be a "positive, ten benefits of staying pure," message. It all fell into place with a couple of illustrations involving student participation. I was so nervous the whole week before that I lost weight. I was to speak to all six health classes each hour of the day. I was amazed during the first class when the students were paying such close attention and responded very well to the talk. I handed out commitment cards to each student at the end of the class. During one class, there was a boy with several piercings and bleached blonde hair pulled back into a pony-tail. This was a new thing at the time. He seemed to fall asleep several times and talked to his friend next to him while I was talking, so I assumed he was getting nothing out of it. When I finished, he was the first to come up to me and thank me. He asked me to sign as his witness on his commitment card, and then asked for a card for his mother! You just never know what God is doing!

"I can do all things through Him who strengthens me."
Philippians 4:13

When I got home that night, exhausted after doing this six times, Larry had made an 8.5 x 11 card for me - what a guy! *(photo pg 53)* This was the beginning of many invitations to speak on abstinence to students in schools and churches. Sometimes I would preach the morning service at churches on abortion and then on abstinence in the evening. I received letters from some of the students thanking me for sharing my story *(letters pg 51 & 52)*. I always started by telling them what happened to me because of the decision I made to not wait: emotional stress, missing a semester of college, three major surgeries, almost dying, and infertility. They appreciated my honesty and felt a connection with me before I shared the 10 reasons to stay pure.

Washington DC

Lynn and I were invited to attend and speak at a conference in Washington DC about abortion. We were able to stay with old army friends - the Flanigans - and participate in this very interesting conference. One of the other speakers was Joan Appleton, who had been a friend of Molly Yard and very involved in the NOW organization. She was a nurse at an abortion clinic because she wanted to help women and thought this would be a good way. There were some pro-life ladies outside the clinic on a regular basis praying for the clients. Joan got to know one of them very well, noticed how loving she was, and that she really cared for the women too. After many years at the clinic and seeing women come back again and again for abortions, she noticed that they were in worse shape each time they came. With the help of the pro-life lady, she was finally able to leave the clinic, and she eventually became a born again Christian. She mentioned how blinded the pro-choice people are - they just can't see all that is happening because of what they are doing. Again, this was proof that love never fails. It was the love of the sidewalk counselor that opened her eyes to see what was really happening.

While in DC, the group of speakers also had the opportunity to protest on the steps of the Supreme Court, holding grave stones with the names of babies that have been aborted *(photo pg 55)*. We also were invited to attend a press conference in front of the Capital with one of our pro-life senators. I felt so honored to be able to be a part of working for this issue. It still amazes me that God turned the worst thing in my life into the most rewarding over and over again.

> "And we know that God causes
> all things to work together for good
> to those who love God,
> to those who are called according to His purpose."
>
> *Romans 8:28*

More Financial Miracles

In 1992, I felt the need to move from the country back into town since Bill was more involved in school and since he would be driving soon. We looked and looked for a house in the Grandville area, but they were all 1,200 square feet with chopped up rooms and back yards with no privacy. I prayed for a home with a private back yard (we were used to no neighbors in the country and loved it), and something more open with more space. I noticed a home in the paper that looked nice, but it was 2,400 square feet on the main floor with a walkout basement on 2.5 acres. I knew it must be $100,000 over our price range. One day I drove past an open house with Betsy and thought it looked like the one in the paper. We went in and the price was only $20,000 over what we wanted to pay. The reason for the price was that it was a dump: carpet worn through to the backing, very old decorating with people on the wallpaper, very dirty, and the landscaping had all been torn out because it had covered up all the windows. It was just cosmetic problems. The layout was great and it had two fireplaces (one marble) with a total of 4,000 square feet. It would be wonderful for all the entertaining that we did. I called Larry and he came right over before the open house ended. It was just 5 minutes from church. He couldn't see it looking nice, but I assured him I could make it nice very easily.

The owner came home and we talked with him for a while and he played his organ for us. He was an 80-year-old widower. After another visit with Bill, we checked with the city about a road assessment that we thought might be coming, and they confirmed there would be a $10,000 assessment in the spring. That news put it out of our range. When we did not make an offer, the owner called our agent and asked her, "Doesn't that nice family want to buy my house?" She told them about the assessment and he said he would pay that! We put our house up for sale by owner and the first couple through made a cash offer that we accepted. We then put together our offer but there were two other offers

80

put in that night. He asked about ours first and even though he knew one of the others was for more, he accepted our offer. It was a miracle!

> "...And my God will supply all your needs
> according to His riches in glory in Christ Jesus."
>
> *Philippians 4:19b*

The second part of the miracle came three years later. The home had a 20-year roof on it that was now 33 years old. We had no money to pay for it and the estimate was $6,000. I had been praying since we bought the house for the money to pay for it. On top of that, I felt God wanted me to take time off from my little job at Karen Deckrow's house on Tuesdays which paid about $80. When I questioned the Lord about this, He said "Do you think your piddley $80 is going to pay for your $6,000 roof? Quit your job and trust me." I called Karen on Monday and told her. Then we asked an acquaintance who is a builder if he would have time to put on our roof. He said he would like to do it with his son and would come take a look and give us a price. Then on Friday, we got a letter in the mail from a deceased missionary's attorney. We had helped her return to the states in her retirement and visited her with the kids. She had left us $5,000! Guess how much the price to do the roof was - not $5,000, but $4,500. That is the $5,000 minus our $500 tithe. God even provided the tithe! What a God we serve!

> "Trust in the LORD and do good;
> dwell in the land and cultivate faithfulness.
> Delight yourself in the LORD;
> and He will give you the desires of your heart."
>
> *Psalm 37:3-4*

I had the opportunity to be a speaker at a conference at Focus on the Family in Colorado Springs. I was also interviewed for their Pastor to Pastor series which sends tapes out to pastors all over the country each month covering various topics. Of course, my topic was abortion and helping those who have had abortions receive healing. I received many phone calls over the years as a result of that interview. One such call was from a wonderful pastor in Illinois right near Six Flags Great America. He wanted me to come and speak to his church. After unsuccessfully trying to encourage him to do it himself, by sending him my notes, Larry and I finally agreed to come. I spoke at the morning service on abortion and healing. Then in the evening they had all the teenagers sit up front and I spoke about abstinence. It was a great day! (flyer pg 53) But one of the neatest things was that we found out that our old John Deere riding mower needed $1,200 in repair work before we came. I was concerned about where the money would come from until God reminded me that He had always supplied our need. I had just resigned from Mourning Joy Ministries (all the money and offerings that I received when I spoke I gave to MJM while there). At dinner after the evening service, the pastor handed me a check for $1,200! He had asked me what I charged before I came. I told him whatever they wanted to give me was fine. If I had given an amount, it would have been much less. I never expected to receive such a large amount, but God always has a plan. The pastor called me three weeks later just to tell me again how much everyone enjoyed the day I was there and that they were still talking about it!

"I am my beloved's and my beloved is mine,..."
Song of Songs 6:3a

In June of 1996, God began to move in a powerful way in our church. There was revival springing up in many churches across the country and beyond, and now it had come to First Assembly. In August, we began Friday night services so that those who attended other churches could experience this without missing their own services. We saw so many miraculous things that I could not begin to write it all here. I will just tell the story of one night when the visiting pastors came forward to be prayed for. Something happened when those praying for them got to the middle of the line (right in front of me). Sam, the evangelist began to "slip" and could hardly stand up. Larry, who was right next to him, also was having a hard time standing up. Finally, the two of them struggled to get to their seats on the platform and sit down. Shortly after the break (because the services ran several hours), a lady caught me on my way to the restroom. She told me that the visitor behind her had seen a cloud raining on Larry and Sam, and it followed them up onto the platform as they walked to their chairs. When I told Pastor Benson this, he said I was the third person to tell him about the cloud. When he asked the congregation after the break if anyone else had seen the cloud, about ten people raised their hands from different areas of the sanctuary. Larry later told me that when he was right in front of me, he saw water coming down on the back of the person Sam was praying for, and that the water was splashing everywhere as Sam was slipping in it. I can't tell you what all of this means, but God was doing something in the life of the pastor being prayed for, and He was certainly showing Himself mighty to me and Larry and Sam.

During the revival, I never had God touch me personally in a physical way, though He did touch many others including Larry more than once. I really wanted to experience something supernatural, and was somewhat disappointed that it didn't happen. In 1998, I felt the Lord wanted me to go to Pensacola (where the revival began in 1995) for the Women's conference in January 1999, but I didn't want to be gone from my family six days, or to spend the money it would cost. I also did not want to go to another service and watch everyone else receive a touch, but not me. After not being able to shake this request from God, I registered with my friend Karen Deckrow. I still did not want to go, and after we attended the first service, I thought it was a nice service, but I didn't "get anything" from God worth coming here for. While lying in bed that night, I began to feel bad about my bad attitude and apologized to God and told Him I would forget about "getting anything" from Him and just worship Him. During the next service in the morning, the worship was wonderful and I fully participated. We were singing songs to God about how much we loved Him and I could truly feel His presence in a special way. Then the worship leader had a word from the Lord which said how much He loved us. I could feel His great love and then suddenly I felt Him hugging me physically! It was so real that I put my arms out to hug Him back, but there wasn't anything there. I just stood there with my eyes closed, my arms across my chest and feeling this wonderful hug and enjoying this incredible moment with the Lord with what was probably a silly grin on my face. Then the Lord said to me, "Averie, I didn't want you to come here to get something from me. I just wanted to be with you, away from the phone, the kids, the responsibilities and distractions so that we could just be together - you and Me!" When worship was finally over, Karen told me to remind her to tell me what she had seen while we were worshipping. I sat down and said to the Lord, "What was that? Was that real or did I just make it up?"

After lunch, Karen and I were in the sanctuary waiting for the service to start, and I told her what the Lord had said to me (she knew that I didn't want to come to this conference). Then she said to me, "Well, that makes what I saw make more sense. I saw you facing me, and then I saw the back of Jesus in a white robe. He lifted His arms and put them around you and hugged you and all I could see of you was your smiling face engulfed in His arms while he hugged you." I couldn't believe that God had shown that to Karen so that I would know that it was real. He knows His children so well!

Trusting God with our Children

The week that revival started at church was also the week that one of our most difficult times as parents began. Bill had always been strong willed and was hard for me to deal with sometimes, but Bill had just begun to take drugs and we did not know it yet. We didn't find out until much later that he was feeling rejected by his biological parents and didn't understand why they "didn't want him." Then the wonderful girl that he was dating broke up with him. He then ran away from home the Friday night after revival started and we had no idea where he was. He came home the next day, but we just were not able to communicate with him at all. Things continued to get worse, and then in September, I felt like God wanted me to fast for 40 days about the situation. I had never done this before - the most I had fasted was 7 days. I told God I would do it, but if I felt too sick or weak at any time, then I would stop. I had no problem completing the 40 day fast, and neither did Larry who decided to do it with me. I didn't get any great revelation during the fast, but I sensed God telling me it was going to get worse before it got better.

The Wednesday before Thanksgiving, I went to pick Bill up after Wednesday night church and found out he never went to the youth group and he was gone. We had no idea where he was. Larry put a suitcase full of his things out on the porch which he picked up sometime the next day. About a week and half later, I was in church and wanted to praise during worship like always, but it seemed so hard when I had no idea what was happening to Bill. God reminded me of Psalm 37:4 and said to me, "Delight yourself in the Lord and He will give you the desires of your heart." My hands went up and I thought, "Not only can I praise you, but I MUST praise you!" A couple more weeks went by with not a word from Bill. He was 17, in his senior year and had dropped out of high school, and missed being on his high school state championship football team after playing football for six years. I didn't know if he was dead or alive.

As I talked to God about it, He told me that I didn't know what was happening or what was going to happen, but He knew the end from the beginning. He knew where we were going, so I should just take His hand and walk with Him, because He knew the way. It was a tremendous comfort to take His hand and trust Him. The first time we heard from Bill was one week before Christmas when he called us from jail. We did not bail him out until a week later when we had worked everything out with the court and Teen Challenge for him to enroll in the one year program there. He completed the program in January of 1998 and had a much better attitude, but he still wasn't living right. There were many ups and downs during the years to come, and the only way we could make it through it all with any sense of peace was by trusting God. I don't know how parents get through things like this without the help of the Lord. I often felt like a failure as a parent, but God finally said to me one day, "I am the perfect parent, and every one of My children has rebelled against me. Do you think you are better than Me?" This helped ease my guilt. We love our children so much and want to do our best for them. It is hard when we can't seem to figure out how.

Not only did we have struggles with Bill, but Betsy also became very difficult when she entered high school. She seemed disgusted by everything I said or did. It was very hard to be so disrespected. At God's direction, I finally told her that whenever she was disrespectful, she would have to do something for me. So, the next time she had a bad attitude, I said, "Thank you Betsy, now I get to have you wash my kitchen floor!" This helped me tremendously.

> "For the LORD gives wisdom;
> from His mouth come knowledge and understanding.
> He stores up sound wisdom for the upright..."
> *Proverbs 2:6-7a*

Encouragement for parents of teenagers

Be encouraged that your teenagers will not be like they are now in another 10 years. They will be much different with a different perspective when they reach their mid-twenties. Now fast-forward 10 years. Bill and Betsy are now in their mid and late 20s and are roommates in an apartment in Grand Rapids. Bill calls me up one night to tell me, "Now I know what it must have been like to have me live with you for 4 years!" (He moved in with us so he could attend U of M and get his graphic design degree). He told me that Betsy was doing this and doing that, and leaving all her dirty dishes around the kitchen. When he was talking to her about it she told him, "You sound like

Mom!" Then Bill said, "Well, maybe Mom was right!" I had to laugh out loud because I never thought I would hear those words come out of Bill's mouth.

Then a couple of years later, I get a call from Betsy around 9 pm on a Tuesday night. She told me that she had just gone out for coffee with a guy she had liked for about a year now. This was the first time they were together alone, just to talk and get to know each other a bit better. She asked Justin if he had a mentor. He said no, but explained how he had learned a lot from his parents. Then he asked Betsy what she was like in high school. She told him that she had been pretty bad and quite rebellious, and that she probably could have learned much from her parents, but missed out on that because of her attitude. Then she said to me, "So, Mom, I called you tonight to tell you that you were not a bad mom, I was a bad daughter." I cannot tell you how much that meant to me, and what healing that statement brought to my heart. I had never met this Justin, but I loved him already. He and Betsy were married almost two years later on June 30, 2012.

To Parents of Challenging Strong-willed Children

From the time I was a little girl, my dream was to be a wife and mother. Even though I had a business degree, had little businesses in my home and was a speaker and teacher, my first love was being a wife and mother. When Betsy graduated from high school, I felt like my training time with my kids was over and I was a failure! Bill was still not living right and Betsy was disgusted by me. At this time, I had lunch with my friend Karen Deckrow. I admired her more than any other mother. She had 5 children and I watched her interact with them when I worked in her home all those years. She was so wise and her kids were great. In the middle of our conversation, she said to me, "Averie, I have to tell you something. I have five children and only one of them is like your two. That one child takes more effort and energy than the other four combined. I cannot imagine having two like that. And what is even more important, I cannot imagine not having at least one easy child so that you knew you were a good mother!" Oh, my gosh! I cannot tell you the healing that brought to my soul. I felt it was God saying to me, "I know you feel like a failure, but you are not. I understand. It is not over yet. Hang in there. Of course, years later I saw huge changes and now have children who are grateful for their family and parents. You can hang in there too, so don't quit!" It is impossible to be a failure if you don't quit.

Chapter IX

A New Millennium
Trusting God for Your Job

It was around 1997 that Larry began to feel like he should leave First Assembly and pastor a church. Larry mentioned it to Pastor Benson and was told he wasn't ready yet. The next year Larry brought it up again and was told it would not be a good time for the church. Finally, the third year in the fall of 1999, Larry told Pastor Benson that he needed to leave and pastor a church. Pastor Benson asked him to wait until he returned from his annual time away with the Lord. When he returned two weeks later, he told Larry that he was leaving. So, instead of us leaving, the Benson's left First Assembly after 25 years, and Larry became the interim pastor for 9 months until the new pastor was selected and arrived.

When Scott Hagan, the newly-elected Pastor arrived from Sacramento, CA, he asked Larry to stay for at least a year to help him get adjusted to the church. Larry agreed. The Monday before Pastor Scott was to arrive, Pastor Krist and a few members of his board at Trinity Assembly of God (near Flint) came to talk to Larry about going through a pastoral transition, since Pastor Krist had announced his retirement the day before. At the end of the meeting, they asked Larry to submit his resume to the Trinity search committee. Larry said he couldn't consider it since he had committed to a year with Pastor Scott Hagan.

Larry received calls from all over the U.S. offering him jobs at big churches, but the only one that stayed with me was Trinity. Their search committee continued to call Larry every month through May, and then July, but Larry told them, "No." every time. In October, Nancy Walker, a member at Trinity saw a vision at the altar when she was praying. She saw a man that she knew was their new pastor, but he was walking away from the church. Then God's hands came down and turned him back toward the church. He said to her that this man would come off the expressway, up the driveway to the church without being called. She asked Dennis Rainwater, the head of the search committee, if the vision meant anything to him and he said, "No."

On December 9, 2001, our church was taping an instructional video for churches involved in pastoral transitions. A panel, including the former and current pastors of First Assembly and Larry, as the interim pastor, were joined by the chairmen of the search committees from Grand Rapids First Assembly and Harvest Church of Sacramento. Ron McManus was the moderator of the discussion. Before the evening service began, Ron had asked Larry how many churches were searching for a new senior pastor in Michigan. Having recently heard the number was 26, he shared it with Ron. In his introduction, Ron told the congregation that statistic, and when he did, I heard the Holy Spirit say to me, "What are you doing here?" Larry felt something similar as well. It was our release from First Assembly. The next morning Pastor Scott told Larry that he felt guilty keeping Larry here when he could be pastoring any church in the country. That was our release from Scott.

That evening we were driving to Frankenmuth for the annual District Missionary Retreat, and I prayed that God would speak to Larry if he was supposed to consider Trinity because it was still on my heart. Ten minutes later, Larry asked if I wanted to drive to Trinity when we reached the exit where it was located. I said, "Sure!" We sat in the parking lot of the church for a minute in the dark and then went on to Frankenmuth. The next day we stopped by again and went inside. The Music Minister told Larry that the committee was interviewing a candidate for the second time that night. We then received a tour of the church and left. As Larry was pulling back onto the expressway, he called Dennis Rainwater to pray with him about the interview that night. Dennis was so excited to hear Larry's voice, and told him that he had been on his mind for the last three days and begged him to submit his resume. Larry felt bad interfering with the current candidate, but after some discussion, he finally agreed. Dennis called Nancy Walker right away and asked her to tell him that vision again. Larry had changed his mind and had driven into Trinity's driveway without getting a call! We came for an interview the next week and then again nine days later.

The first Sunday in January, Larry received a call asking him to be their candidate for Trinity's new pastor. The date was set for February 3, 2002. We had several interviews and meals with the elders and deacons, the pastors, and the members on Friday and Saturday. On Sunday, Larry preached the morning and evening services, and a vote was taken. The vote was 97% "yes!" We were installed on March 24, 2002 (photo pg 55). The vision that God gave Nancy was a huge blessing to us. It really helped us know for sure that this was God's plan for us, and we humbly accepted it.

Trusting God During Transition

Being a pastor's wife is one thing, but being a senior pastor's wife is another thing. Every church has critical negative people, and we would be in the spotlight constantly. Because of my background of insecurity, I asked God to help me at this new church. I didn't want to take the negative things personally and let it get me down. I needed His divine help to keep my eyes on Him and His call for Larry and me to this congregation. God is so faithful. For almost three years, I felt like I had a supernatural oil all over me. When the criticism came, which it always does when you follow a pastor of 23 years, it just slid right off me. I didn't feel it. When the oil lifted in January of 2005, I was okay because

I knew I had lived through 3 years of it, God was with me and it was okay. Of course, Larry and I always check ourselves to see if the criticism is legitimate so we can respond properly to it, but many times it is not, and you just have to let it go. Remember - just love them, as God had always told me since the day I met Him!

> "...Obey My voice, and I will be your God,
> and you will be my people;
> and you will walk in all the way which I command you,
> that it may be well with you."
>
> *Jeremiah 7:23b*

The next part of the transition to Trinity that I faced was: What does God want me to do here? What ministry does He want me involved in? The former pastor's wife had been extremely involved in the running of the church and a big part of that was heading up the Women's Ministry. I had no desire or talent to take over that ministry. It just sounded so overwhelming to me. I had no clue how to do it. I prayed for three months about it. During that time, I was adjusting to a new city that I was unfamiliar with, 600 people that I didn't know yet and needed to learn their names, while all my things were still in our G.R. home that had not sold yet. We were living in an apartment over a garage for one month, and then in someone's empty house for two months. I felt kind of like I was in a dream.

Then, a couple of weeks after we sold our home and moved into our new home and got settled, God spoke to me. I had knelt to pray about the sermon at the end of the service that Sunday morning, but instead of praying about that, when I closed my eyes, I saw a chart with "Women of the Word, Women of the Spirit, Women of Fellowship, Women of Mission, Women of Freedom, Women of Worship, Women of Excellence." I knew immediately that God was asking me to head the Women's Ministry and I was to call it Women of Trinity. I was to get a woman from the church to head up each category, and I would oversee the whole thing. Well, with it all organized like that for me, it didn't seem so overwhelming and I was able to obey God without fear, even though I still had no desire to do it and did not feel qualified. God knew how good this would be for me personally, and for the church. I am so glad that I led the women at Trinity for those twelve years. It truly helped me get to know them, and helped them get to know me. However, I would have gladly handed it over to someone that was a good leader with a burden for this ministry, but that "someone" never appeared. Once again God had stretched me and caused me to grow in a new area. He is so good at that, but He never forces us. We must be willing to obey, and when we do, we will always be blessed tremendously!

> "...Our adequacy is from God,
> who also made us adequate as servants..."
>
> *2 Corinthians 3:5-6*

Neighborhood Bible Study

After we settled into our new house, I felt that God wanted me to eventually hold a neighborhood Bible study in my home. I knew that I would be doing it at some point but did not look forward to going around the neighborhood and inviting people. You never know how you will be received. Finally, in April of 2005, I was doing my devotions at my desk, when suddenly I heard God speak to me so clearly. He told me to do the Bible study NOW! It was so clear that I closed my Bible and began typing an invitation that I could leave at the homes where no one answered the door.

> "Be diligent to present yourself
> approved to God as a workman
> who does not need to be ashamed,
> accurately handling the word of truth."
>
> *2 Timothy 2:15*

I found that Saturday afternoons seemed to be a good time to catch people at home, so for the next four Saturdays, I went to all 150 homes in our subdivision. I really enjoyed meeting so many people in my neighborhood. Most were very nice and almost everyone had a huge dog or two that would greet me. I ended up with fifteen ladies that said they were interested. In August, when it was time to buy the books, there were seven who could commit to coming. I went to the Christian bookstore and looked through the Bible studies that they had available. I chose a very basic one called "Receiving God's Love". There was a little bit of homework in the book that we would discuss each week. The ladies really enjoyed it.

For the spring of 2006, they decided they were ready to tackle a Beth Moore study which would involve more homework than the first study. It was called "Jesus, the One and Only". They loved the study and Beth Moore! Since then we have also done "The Patriarchs", "Daniel", "Believing God" (my personal favorite), "A Woman's Heart, God's Dwelling Place", "Living Beyond Yourself (Fruit of the Spirit)", "Esther", "The Psalms of Ascent", "Loving Well", "Breaking Free", "The Truth Project", "Revelation", "James", "Malachi", "The Bible in 90 Days" and "When Wallflowers Dance". We usually had 8-10 there on Thursday mornings. (photo pg 55)

Rosemary, the second from the left, told us a great story after she had been coming two years. She shared how she was considering leaving her marriage because she had been unhappy for quite a while. She had even picked out a small house to buy for her and the kids, and she would let her lawyer husband keep the big house. She had given her life to God when she was 14, but had not been to church. She prayed for God to show her what to do before she made her final decision. Then I showed up at her door to invite her to the Bible study, and she knew God had sent me. She was thrilled to come to the study and it completely changed her life. She said that the past year had been the best ever for her marriage. One day when her husband asked her why Jesus was so important to her now, she said to him, "You know how our

94

marriage has been so good this past year? Well, it is all because of Him." I had no idea how important it was that I start the Bible study NOW like God said. I have learned to be obedient, because God always knows what He is doing! Rosemary shared some other great things God has done in her life, and then, when her husband landed a new job, she moved with her family to Minnesota. We missed her very much!

"All Scripture is inspired by God and profitable for teaching, for reproof, for correction, for training in righteousness; so that the man of God may be adequate, equipped for every good work."

2 Timothy 3:16-17

The Philippines

In early 2006, I learned that Mary Selzer (Michigan District Women's Ministry Leader) was looking for pastor's wives to join a team to go to the Philippines to teach a Pastor's wives conference. The wives there had never had anything like this before, so the missionary invited us to come. I had no desire to go. I do not like the 12-hour time change at all, and I didn't want to go that far away without Larry. Also, it would be very hot and humid with no air conditioning, and I get sick in that kind of heat. Well, God kept reminding me of this trip and I felt like He wanted me to go, but I did not want to do it. Besides, I did not have the $2,000 that it cost, so I felt justified. In May, I was looking at the District Council schedule and noticed a meeting for this trip. I had received a check from Mom a week or so before this that would cover the cost, so I no longer had a lack of money as an excuse (even though I would rather spend the money on something else.) While I sat in the meeting, my heart began pounding as the Lord spoke to me exactly what I was to speak on at the conference - the marriage relationship and "Great Fruitfulness Lies on the Other Side of Great Sacrifice". The decision was made, and on July 24, the eight of us left for the Philippines. We arrived at our "guest house" in Manila around 1:30 am on the 26th and had to get up to catch our flight to the retreat center at 4:30 am. We arrived in time for lunch and then the conference began that afternoon. We held an opening service that Mary spoke at. We then held workshops with each of us teaching a different topic. This is when I taught on marriage. I taught them the Biblical role of the husband and the wife, and then shared how Jesus had elevated the status of women when He came to this earth. Women were treated like dogs at that time, and Jesus' treatment of women with dignity and value was radical!

Later, on the weekend when each of us went home with a different pastor and his wife to preach in their churches, one of the wives in my workshop read all her notes to her husband. After listening to it all, he said, "Well, we are going to have to change a lot of things around here!" You see, the culture in that area of the Philippines believed that husbands are allowed to beat their wives - there is nothing wrong with it. When we had devotions with the wives each day, many wives asked for prayer because their husbands beat them. Even though they were pastors, they had not yet learned what the Bible teaches about marriage! Now I could see why I felt the Holy Spirit telling me so strongly to teach on this. Thank you, God, for once again using me to help others!

It was very hot and humid as expected, but we had window air conditioners in our rooms where we slept, which was unexpected. Praise the Lord! The next morning, we were each given a group of the wives to have devotions with before breakfast. We had a morning and evening service on Thursday with Carol and Shelly preaching the messages, and then two more sessions of workshops. Friday morning was the closing service which I preached – "Great Fruitfulness Lies on the Other Side of Great Sacrifice" *(photo pg 56).* I felt sweat running down my back the whole time because of the heat. I was concerned that my message was too hard for these women who already have it so hard, but all 120 of them came to the altar to pray at the end of the message. Debbie, the missionary, had tears in her eyes and said it was a perfect word for the ladies. Thank you Lord for your awesome guidance! We spent the afternoon checking into a hotel, shopping, and visiting a Bible School. Then on Saturday, we were all picked up by different pastors and their wives and taken to their homes for the weekend. I went to the base of a mountain with a former District Superintendent. I taught a workshop on marriage to the ladies of several churches that afternoon. After eating dinner and spending the night in their home, we went to church for the Sunday service and I preached again.

After lunch, we then drove up the mountain a couple of hours and I preached the afternoon service at a tiny bamboo church *(photo pg 56)*. At the end of this service I felt the Holy Spirit tell me to give the pastor my notebook with the notes for my three sermons in it. He took it and with tears opened it and rubbed his hands on the marriage notes and said, "We need this so badly here." Then he turned to the Fruitfulness notes and said, "This is such a powerful word!" He was so grateful for the gift. What an incredible experience this all was. It is amazing that God can use an insignificant vessel like me to minister to people half way around the world. Again, obedience is always the best policy.

My Sunshine

Soon after we arrived at Trinity, Bill informed us that he was expecting a child with the girl he had broken up with a couple of months earlier. The baby was to be born in December. Larry and I were so disappointed, to say the least. It took me about a week or so to adjust to the idea as I realized that this was my first grandchild. It took Larry a lot longer to get over his anger, but by the time Kaylee was born on December 1, 2002, he was smitten with his granddaughter just like I was. We were there when she was born and we went to Grand Rapids as often as we could to see her. We had her come and stay with us a week at a time, and we could have her with us for every holiday then as well. Then Bill gave his life to God on Mother's Day 2005 at the altar at Trinity. Three weeks later he moved in with us so that he could attend U of M Flint and get his degree. He soon gained shared custody of Kaylee and we were blessed to have her live with us half the time for the next four years. Kaylee has been such a blessing to me personally *(photo pg 59)*. She has always had such a sweet spirit and she is so teachable. She has a will, but not the very strong will that Bill and Betsy had. It was such a joy to have her with us. She became the light of my life - my sunshine, which I sing to her often. She and Bill were with us for four years, and then they moved back to Grand Rapids. I missed her so, but she came to stay with us every summer for a few weeks and during many of her school vacations. God certainly does work all things for good to those who love God and are called according to His purpose. (Romans 8:28). Thank you again, God, for your incredible blessings!

Disney World Vacation

Remember when back in 1988, we canceled our trip to Disney World to make our $20,000 pledge to the new sanctuary? Well, in 2009, General Council was held in Orlando. We had been thinking about taking Kaylee to Disney World, so we flew Bill and Kaylee down after council was over. We were able to get a suite at the Marriott Resort right across from Sea World for $25 a night! It was beautiful and had 6 swimming pools. What fun! We went to the Magic Kingdom on Monday after planning carefully the night before how to get the most out of our day from all that we read on the internet. We arrived at 7:30 am and there were only 3 cars in the parking lot. We didn't need to catch a tram so we just walked to the monorail and arrived at the Magic Kingdom at 7:40 (Main Street opened at 8:30 and the park opened at 9).

A lady kept getting in a picture I was trying to take of Kaylee in front of the landscape that was shaped like Mickey Mouse. I asked her to move so I could get Mickey in the photo, but she said I would get a much better picture of Mickey if she were in my picture. I took the picture and finally she told us that we were going to help Mickey open the park. We were taken immediately into the park and Kaylee was allowed to pick out a pen and autograph book. They drove us past the castle to Toon

Town in a 1908 Model T. We toured Mickey and Minnie's house and then one by one all the characters came out to greet us. We couldn't believe this was happening *(photos pg 57)*! After a time with the characters we all walked down to the train and rode it to above the park gate where we waved and greeted all those entering the park with Mickey and the dancers. A photographer then took a photo of us with Mickey. We spent 45 minutes in the park alone. What an incredible experience! The day after we got home, I was telling the Lord how wonderful it had been and asking Him "why were we so blessed?" He said to me, "Remember 21 years ago when you gave up your trip to Disney World? Well, I gave it back, but I made it better!"

Ministry Opportunities

After coming to Flint, I thought maybe I would quit my Creative Memories business that I had been doing for 5 years. Larry suggested that it would be a good way to get to know a lot of the ladies in the church. I didn't want them to think I just wanted to sell them something. Well, it turned out that several ladies really wanted to learn how to scrapbook and asked to hold or attend a class. It did turn out to be a great opportunity to spend time with many of them. I then remembered one of my customers in G.R. who was working on albums of her husband who had died recently. She was 80 years old and she thanked me so much for my "ministry."

When I first arrived in Flint, I had to find somewhere to get my nails done. Having no idea where to go, I drove up and down Pierson Rd. looking and praying for a place. The first place did not feel right. Another place had the word Unisex on their sign and that just didn't sound good to me. After quite a while, I felt God wanted me to go into Sergio's (with the word unisex). I sat down with Gina, and when she found out Larry was a pastor, she immediately began asking me all kinds of spiritual questions. She began to look forward to our time together every two weeks and would even have her sister Debbie (the owner) come over and hear some of the stories I was telling about the Lord. Well, it had been about three years, and she had never prayed the salvation prayer. I asked God why because she seemed so ready. Finally, 3 weeks later she told me how she was driving to work and began praying her own prayer instead of her Catholic prayers. She asked God to forgive her of all her sins and she gave her life to Him and said she started to cry and felt tingly. Then she asked me what had happened. I told her "you are born again!" She was so hungry for God and grew so much the following years. Nothing is better than this - to help someone find a personal relationship with Jesus *(photo pg 59)*!

About Angels

On August 3, 2010 I had my hip replaced at McLaren Medical Center. When I came home from the hospital, Mom, then 87 years old, came to take care of me for a few days because I wasn't able to do much. Just getting to the bathroom was a big deal. On Sunday, 3 days after I got home, I woke up at 7:00 am. Mom was sleeping in the bed with me and Larry had gone to church, as he always does on Sundays, at 4:00 am. I got up to go do my devotions in the living room. We had fixed a special chair with extra pillows on it for me, because I was not allowed to bend past 90 degrees for 6 weeks. When I had gotten half way to the chair, I began to get dizzy and knew I was going to faint. I went as fast as I could with my walker, which wasn't very fast, saying, "Help me Jesus, help me Jesus...", as I went. I almost reached the fireplace near the ottoman in front of the chair when I passed out. When I woke up later, I was lying perfectly with my head and shoulders on the cushion of the chair and my bottom and legs on the ottoman. As I gained my senses, I looked and saw the walker knocked over way on the other side of the ottoman where I passed out. I could never have fallen from there to where I was. As I lay there confused, I asked the Lord how I got there. I heard Him say, "I had my angel catch you and lay you here." WOW! I felt so loved and cared for. That is exactly like our God. He is always there to catch us when we fall if we love and trust Him! If I had fallen, my hip would have dislodged and I would have had to have the surgery all over again. Thank you, Lord! You are so awesome!

> "For He will give His angels charge concerning you,
> to guard you in all your ways."
>
> *Psalm 91:11*

Honoring your parents

When my mom was turning 75, we had a big birthday party for her at the country club. As I was trying to figure out what gift to give her, I felt God wanted me to honor her. I found all the photos I could of her while I was growing up (there weren't many) and tried to think of all the positive things about Mom to put into a little 5x7 album. I had carried a lot of hurt inside over the years and God wanted me to let it all go. I made a wonderful album, and on the last page told her that even though I was not the perfect daughter and she was not the perfect mom, I was so glad God had given me her to be my mom.

> "Honor your Father and Mother
> (which is the first commandment with a promise.)"
>
> *Ephesians 6:2*

The party was very nice, and my lawyer brother and Mom's wealthy friends were all giving her expensive gifts. I was getting embarrassed about my gift which she hadn't opened yet. Well, she finally opened the album and her friend across the table from me said, "Averie, that is the best gift!" Then the next morning, Mom called to tell me again how much she loved her album. She had read it 3 times the night before and was reading it again that morning. After that, our relationship has been much closer. It is amazing what such a small thing can accomplish.

Here is one more thing about Mom. I love to entertain and we are constantly having people and groups over to our home. I enjoy cooking and treating them special. Well, a couple of years ago, I was setting the table for the Christmas dinner I cook for my Women of Trinity board (10 ladies) every December. As I was walking around setting the table, God spoke to my heart that I love to do this and learned to do this by watching my mom do the same thing while I was growing up. No one had taught me how to entertain, but I had watched my mom joyfully do this constantly all those years when I was young. I was naturally doing what I had observed and learned from her. I consider it a special gift that she has given me.

God is Always with Us

"God is our refuge and strength,
A very present help in trouble.
Therefore we will not fear, though the earth should change
and though the mountains slip into the heart of the sea;"

Psalm 46:1-2

In 2008, Larry and I took a mission trip to the Congo to help Gary and Jan Dickinson. We had a wonderful time with them and while there Jan shared this story with me. When they first came to Africa as missionaries, they were in Kinshasa in the Democratic Republic of Congo (it may have been Zaire at the time). They established a church, raised up leaders and trained a pastor. Things were going very well, but a revolt took place as the government was crushed and a new tribe took over. They could hear the screams, and the shooting and fighting all around them from their house as the new regime was ravaging the city. The homes there were all surrounded by big concrete walls with gates. They took their two young daughters up to the attic and prayed that when they broke into their home they would not find them up there. Jan told me that she was so angry with God for allowing this. After all, they had given up everything and left home and family to come to this place. How could He let this happen? Well, no one broke into their home and they were able to escape the country and eventually established a new church in the Republic of Congo in Pointe Noire. Jan was still angry with God and didn't quite trust Him the same now.

Fast forward seven years. Gary and Jan were back in the U.S. itinerating on furlough. They were at a church in Ohio where Gary preached the sermon. After the service, a woman came up to Jan and introduced herself. She said "I don't know if this will mean anything to you, but seven years ago, God woke me up in the middle of the night and told me to pray. I didn't know who I was praying for so I prayed in the Spirit. As I was praying in the Spirit I saw you and your husband. It looked like you were in an attic with two little girls. I was standing outside the gate to the house and I had a sword in my hand. Every time someone tried to get in the gate I killed them with my sword. Does that mean anything to you?" Well, needless to say that certainly did mean something to Jan. She told me that she has never doubted God again, and she now knows that God always knows exactly where we are and what is happening, and He is doing exactly what needs to be done, whether I can see what He is doing or not. What a faith builder! We all need to know that ourselves.

The Stephen Morin Story

Recently I had a brand new Christian ask me if people who kill and rape can be saved. I shared this story with her that I heard on Focus on the Family many years ago. In 1982 Margy Mayfield had stopped at K-Mart in San Antonio, Texas to pick up a few things on her way home one day at 2:00 in the afternoon. As she approached her car she felt a gun in her back and turned and saw a crazy man. She asked him if he knew Jesus Christ and then he said, "No, get in the car."

What she did not know was that the whole city was looking for this man because he had kidnapped, raped, and murdered a girl at 2:00 am that morning. He was on the FBI's most wanted list for 10 years and was wanted in many states for rape and murder. He made Margy sit on her hands in the passenger's seat. He was crying and shaking telling her how he was running and didn't know what to do. She told him she was going to pray for him and he said not to. She put her hands on him and prayed for him anyway and took dominion over the demonic spirits and claimed him for Jesus.

"Do not fear those who kill the body
but are unable to kill the soul;
but rather fear Him who is able
to destroy both soul and body in hell."

Matthew 10:28

He said, "I can't believe I'm in the car with a religious fanatic. You don't have to sit on your hands anymore." Then began many hours of her talking to him about God, salvation, and forgiveness. He was shocked by her calmness and lack of fear and she told him there is no fear in God's love. They went many places like What a Burger for food, the bank to get him money, 7-11 to get a newspaper, etc. He told her that he was never going back to prison and she told him that he was already in prison – he agreed. He said he knew the force of Satan that she was talking about, but that he felt a love in her that he had never felt before. She told him he could be a new creature in Christ. All of this took place over many hours that afternoon and evening. The Holy Spirit led her to drive to Kerrville to get him to a bus station because he wanted to get to Fort Worth.

While driving there, she played a Christian preaching tape. She told him more about God's love and forgiveness and he suddenly pulled the car over to the side of the road and put his hands in the air and told Jesus he was sorry for what he had done and asked for forgiveness and cried. Then he said, "it's gone!" She asked him "what is gone?" He said that the hate and anger was gone and he didn't feel like the same person any more. He hugged her and cried on her shoulder. Then he emptied his bullets into her purse.

They ended up at the bus station and she gave him her little book of scripture she had with her and told him to read it and speak it while he rode the bus to Austin and then Ft. Worth. She left and ended up back at home around 10:30 pm. The police were at her house because her husband was worried that she'd been kidnapped. When she drove up he was mad because he thought that she hadn't been with the murderer. Then, when she emptied the bullets from his gun in her purse, he fell to the ground.

She eventually told the police that he should be in Austin bus station by now, waiting to go to Ft. Worth, reading a book of scripture. They laughed and said there was no way someone evading the FBI for 10 years would be that stupid. But they decided to go and there he was, reading the book. He surrendered and was arrested, tried, convicted, and sentenced to death. He asked to see Margy before he was put to death, so she went at the Spirit's bidding even though she didn't want to go in a prison. When she got to the prison, the warden told her that they all loved Stephen and were very sad that he was going to die. Stephen had led him to the Lord and many other guards and prisoners as well. When she saw him, he told her that he was wondering if everything that had happened was real, and asked God to let him see her on his birthday if it was. That day was his birthday and because she came his prayer was answered. This story has encouraged me not to fear, but to turn to God and His leading in every situation! We never know when God will want to use us to minister to someone else, no matter who they are or what they have done. God loves everyone!

Friends Can Make a Huge Difference in Your Life

Many people have had a spiritual impact on my life, including some of the teachers and preachers that I have been blessed to hear. Friends like Georgianna and Lorraine have been a blessing as well.

Ron and Vicky Smit have both loved me just as I am and appreciated my gifts. We have the best talks about spiritual things when we are together. I treasure their friendship and look forward to spending more time with them in the future *(photo pg 58)*.

Of course, Wayne and Kathy Benson *(photo pg 58)* have had a huge impact on both Larry and me as wonderful mentors. We are so thankful that God allowed us to be under their leadership for so many years. Much of what we are and do today is a result of their influence upon our lives.

Thank you, Ron, Vicky, Wayne and Kathy!!!

One Last Story

Our daughter Betsy and Justin, her husband, were expecting a baby on November 24th of 2013. However, Betsy was diagnosed with preeclampsia around August 15th and put into the hospital on August 20th so they could keep an eye on her. The doctors were hoping Betsy could make it another 2-3 weeks before delivering so the baby could continue to develop and grow. She only made it three days before they had to take him to save Betsy's life. He weighed 1 pound and 5 ounces. He was so tiny and hooked up to so many tubes and wires and machines. The goal was for him to be home by his due date. I told Betsy that we can't always know why things happen the way they do, but we can know that God sees a much bigger picture than we do, and He is doing things that we cannot see.

Several weeks later, we got the placenta report and found out that the placenta was sick and worthless. Little Jaxon was not getting the nourishment that he needed and would have died and miscarried if he was not taken when he was due to Betsy's condition. Her preeclampsia saved his life! We serve an awesome God! On April 14, 2014 Jaxon was still in the hospital NICU *(photo pg 59)*.

To All Who Read This Book

When I realized that my children were not aware of all that God had done in Larry's and my life, I felt compelled to write it down so that it would not be lost forever. There are stories yet to be written and some that are not included in this book, but hopefully you can see what an awesome God we serve!

Psalm 78: 1-4, 5b-7, "Listen, O my people, to my instruction; incline your ears to the words of my mouth. I will open my mouth in a parable; I will utter dark sayings of old, which we have heard and known, and our fathers have told us. We will not conceal them from their children, but tell to the generation to come the praises of the LORD, and His strength and His wondrous works that He has done.....He commanded our fathers that they should teach them to their children, that the generation to come might know, even the children yet to be born, that they may arise and tell them to their children, that they should put their confidence in God and not forget the works of God, but keep His commandments."

Love God, obey Him, and love others with His Love!

Updates – August 2017

1. Our Grandson, Jaxon

Jaxon did make it home on oxygen and with a feeding tube about a month after this book first went to print in 2014. In July 2016, after having therapy several days a week since he came home, Jaxon still could not stand, walk, eat food by mouth or say words. He was given the opportunity to be a part of a study at the Conductive Learning Center (only 3 in the world) about 3 miles from our house. At the end of the study 4 weeks later, Jaxon could stand and take steps by himself, eat some food by mouth, was saying words, and had shown drastic improvement in his fine motor skills and comprehension! He is now (August 2017) running everywhere, saying sentences, counting, saying his ABCs and developing more every week. Praise our wonderful Lord! See him with his 2-year-old brother, Olli *(photos next page)*.

2. Don't Forget to be Grateful!

Years ago, I was trying to learn my part in a song that the pastor's wives were to sing at a special service at church. I have a very low voice for a woman (tenor) so I was having a terrible time trying to sing it. Most of the other wives had beautiful voices, but here I was, unable to sing my part correctly. I had tears in my eyes when Larry walked in the door. He looked at me and asked, "What's wrong?" After I told him, he said to me, "Well, Averie, you could have been born in Ethiopia starving to death, but instead, you were born in the U.S. with a low voice." Suddenly, I snapped out of my "feeling sorry for myself" and began to be grateful for my countless blessings. Oh, may we continually give thanks for the multitude of blessings that we have been given! We take so much for granted, and thus miss out on what we actually have.

TOP: Grandsons Olli & Jaxon (always a good squeeze.)

LEFT: Granddaughter, Kaylee (taller than me at 14)